Three Cheers For Ghana!

2nd Edition

Three Cheers For Ghana!

2nd Edition

Robert Peprah-Gyamfi

PERSEVERANCE BOOKS

Three Cheers For Ghana
2nd Edition
First published in 2008 by iUniverse
2021 Pine Lake Road, Suite 100
Lincoln, NE 68512, USA

Published by Perseverance Books
Divine Favour Enterprises Ltd
Loughborough,
LE11 2FB
UK

www: peprah-gyamfi.com
Email: info@peprah-gyamfi.com

Cover design by Isaac Kofi Quansah

ISBN: 978-0-9955524-4-9

To the common man and woman on the streets of Accra and elsewhere in Ghana—may the decision makers of our beloved Ghana remember you always in their deliberations.

Contents

FOREWORD TO THE
SECOND EDITION

M uch has happened in Ghana since I put a final full stop to the first edition of *THREE CHEERS FOR GHANA*, an account of the experience my family and I had during our five weeks' stay in Ghana beginning July 19, 2007.

In the political scene, President John Kofi Agyekum Kufuor's National Patriotic Party (NPP), which was not only in charge of the Presidency but also enjoyed the majority in parliament, lost both the presidential and parliamentary elections held in December 2008 to the opposition National Democratic Congress (NDC).

As far as President Kufuor was concerned, the defeat of his party in the presidential election did not represent a loss to him personally; having served his two terms in office, he was barred by the constitution from standing for a third term. It was rather his party friend, Nana Addo Dankwa Akufo-Addo, who sought to succeed him, who lost to the candidate of the opposition NDC, Prof John Evans Fiifi Atta Mills, in a closely contested race.

Following a peaceful transition of power, Prof Atta Mills assumed the reins of office of the Presidency on January 7, 2009. Sadly, after exercising the power of the Presidency for almost three and a half years, he succumbed to the inevitable foe of humanity on July 24, 2012. It was the first time that a sitting president of the country had died in office. Would the constitution stand the test? Yes, it did indeed.

Hours after the sad event was officially announced, the then vice-president Mr John Dramani Mahama was sworn into the office of the

Presidency in keeping with the constitution. President Mahama in turn selected Mr. Kwesi Amissah-Arthur to serve as Vice-President

Presidential and Parliamentary elections that were due in December of that year went ahead as planned.

The results of the election which was conducted in a generally peaceful atmosphere were contested by the defeated NPP. Eventually, the NPP brought the matter to the Supreme Court. Protracted judicial hearings concerning the case followed which lasted for about four months.

Finally, on August 29, 2013, the Supreme Court upheld the original results, declaring President John Dramani Mahama "validly elected", dismissing all claims of voter fraud, mismanagement and irregularities in the December 2012 Presidential election.

The NPP accepted the ruling, defusing what had been a very charged political atmosphere.

In 2016, after being in power for eight years, the NDC lost both the Presidential and Parliamentary vote to the NPP regime.

Nana Akuffo Addo, who had made two previous unsuccessful attempts at the Presidency, was elected President – 'Three times lucky,' as the English would say! Thus, for over a decade that has passed since our visit to Ghana, things have been fairly quiet and stable on the political front.

However, the situation is not that clear cut when it comes to the matter of the economy.

As readers will later note in my account of our visit, at the time of our arrival in Ghana in July 2007, the country had just undergone a currency recalibration exercise. In the process, four zeros were wiped off the Old Cedi. The new currency was named the Ghana Cedi (GHC). In other words, 10 000 (ten thousand) Old Cedis became 1 Ghana Cedi.

Doing away with the four zeros led the new currency, the Ghana Cedi, to be almost on a par with the US dollar – actually even a bit stronger than the US currency. Indeed, at the time of our arrival, we received 98 Ghana Cedis for the 100 dollars we exchanged in the vicinity of the international airport.

Concerning the UK currency we brought with us, £1 fetched us around GHC1.89.

As I sat down to write these lines on July 7, 2017, I went online to check the latest exchange rate of the Ghana Cedi against the two currencies just referred to. These are the rates that came up: £1 = 5.70 GHC; 1USD = GHC 4.42.

One can deduce from the above figures that the Ghana Cedi has lost about two-thirds of its value against the pound within a decade. As against the US dollar, it is worth about a fifth of what it used to be ten years ago.

Currently, the country heavily depends on importation of goods of various kinds. One might deduce, based on the foreign exchange figures, that the prices of goods are distinctly higher now than they used to be during my visit in 2007 – and that precisely is the case.

I am not an economist; neither am I an expert in the area of foreign exchange mechanisms and determinants.

For reasons that I shall not disclose here, I decided to do my apprenticeship with the group of men and women who are usually referred to in Germany as *die "Götter" im weißen Kittel* (the little gods in white coats).

Though I did not manage to make it to celebrity status in the medical profession, I nevertheless believe I am at home with the basics of my vocation.

Thus, when you approach me with your teenage boy who has over the last several hours been complaining of abdominal discomfort, indeed, who has been complaining of pain that began somewhere around the belly button or navel and has now travelled down "south west", becoming more prominent in the right lower abdomen, and which is associated with nausea (feeling like vomiting) and even actually vomiting, all of this accompanied by a fairly raised temperature, I will surely be certain as to the underlying cause of his problem – though I may choose not to reveal my thoughts to the concerned parents without first properly examining the youngster.

If I do examine my patient – among other things pressing my palm against his right lower abdomen so that the poor guy begins to frown his face in response to the triggered pain – I will surely have the confirmation that I seek, and based on my findings I would be fairly correct to surmise that I suspect the juvenile is afflicted by what the medical world refers to as appendicitis. For the layman reading this, suffice it to know that the condition involves the inflammation of a small tube-shaped sac attached to the lower end of the large intestine.

Now consider, if that lad happens to live in a modern city the likes of Hannover in Germany! (Bless the medical school of that city for offering a deprived peasant farmer's son from one of the most impoverished spots on planet earth the opportunity to learn the vocation I have just referred to!). Or consider the advantage of being in London, formerly the capital of the British Empire and presently of the UK; or in New York, the Headquarters of the United Nations (that is rarely united on pressing issues facing mankind) or any of the advanced countries of the world, which count as the First World Districts of Planet Earth. Indeed, if the afflicted boy happens to live in one of the wealthy countries of the world, he could with all certainty reckon with a speedy medical intervention to his problem, irrespective of the medical system prevailing in his place of residence – whether it is christened the German Krankenkasse, the British NHS, Obamacare (also known as Trumpcare or what have you!).

If, on the other hand, that lad happens to reside in a remote area of the globe the likes of Mpintimpi, the little village in the Eastern Region of Ghana where the placenta or afterbirth of the big-headed, big mouthed, writer of these lines is buried, that lad could indeed face a real threat of seeing his allotted stay on earth terminated even before he could settle down to make long-term plans for the future.

Please do not accuse the writer of trying to blow the matter out of proportion, for whereas it is generally agreed by members of my profession that an appendix has no vital role to play in the human body, it can nevertheless have serious repercussions – when for any reason it goes bonkers or becomes upset or angry or out of sync with the rest of the body and becomes inflamed; for then it could end up exploding or bursting, thereby discharging bowel contents into the space surrounding the belly, which in turn could lead to the poisoning of the body system, a situation which in the worst case scenario, could lead to the death of the individual.

Should the delay in getting medical treatment for the patient in my beloved little Mpintimpi lead to his death, relatives could soon begin pointing accusing fingers at other members of the extended family, in particular the elderly among them, for having used diabolical supernatural powers – witchcraft – to cause the death of the poor lad.

However, I better return to where I left off – to avoid being accused by the experts, the likes of those who engage in literary criticism for a living, of unwarranted digression from the original topic!

So back to where I left! As I declared earlier, I am not an expert in the area of economics. Still, I dare conclude with reasonable certainty that, if only on account of the current exchange rate of the Ghana Cedi with the major international currencies, the economy of my country of birth is not in the reasonably good shape it used to be in ten years before.

That no doubt is the case. Though I do not reside there myself, indeed, though I am writing these lines in the relative comfort of my home in Loughborough in the East Midland region of the former colonial masters of my native Ghana (formerly the Gold Coast colony of the British Empire), the fact is clear, that the cost of living today is far higher than it used to be ten years ago, and this is borne out by the reports that reach me daily via the likes of Facebook, Facet Notebook, Twitter, Twatter, You Tube, My Pipeline, Instagram, Expressgram… you can go on naming all the platforms, forums, social media enclaves in circulation in the Cyber universe!

Talking about the challenges facing Ghana on the economic front could lead one to confront me with the question: 'Is your country of birth devoid of the experts capable of sorting the problems?'

My reply is simple: 'No, my country does not lack the expertise – indeed we boast of a reasonably good number of them.'

'If that is the case,' my imaginary interrogator might say, 'why are they not managing to fix the economy, to ensure that the common man and woman on the streets of "Sodom and Gomorrah" are in good hands?'

That imagined reply has nothing to do with the mincing of words on my part, for indeed a suburb of the capital, Accra, home to the poor and destitute, made up in the main of young men and women who have left the serene surroundings of their villages in search of non-existing jobs in the capital, bears exactly that notorious Biblical Name! So, the question of my imaginary interrogator from this region is: "Do we have to struggle and struggle, day in and day out, in vain to make ends meet?"

Surely, the Foreword of a book is not the proper forum to deal with the complex issue of economics of a nation state. Touching on the matter very superficially, I must concede that some of the factors contributing to the economic decline of my country of birth are home-made. Eradicate corruption, eliminate self-seeking and dishonest public servants, do away with widespread embezzlement of public funds, etc., etc., and the problem will surely be mitigated if not eliminated.

There are external forces at work though! This brings to my mind a claim made by someone I met casually on the street of Accra during my visit there not long ago. Somehow, I joined the stranger in a discussion that centred on the economy, in particular on the falling cedi.

"My friend," he said when I cited economic mismanagement as the main cause of the problem, "don't put all the blame on our economists. We surely have a good number of brilliant economists around. The problem however is that the *system* is simply against us."

"What do you mean by that?" I inquired.

"Well, have you ever noticed the currency of a developing country anywhere in the world being able to compete with those of the advanced countries, the likes of the US, Germany, the UK, and Japan? Can you indeed, mention any currency of the developing world that enjoys a stable rate of exchange compared to the US Dollar, the Euro, the British Pound, the Japanese yen? I do repeat – the system is just against us. So take it from me – no matter the steps a developing country like Ghana may put in place to ensure a stable exchange rate, it will lead to nothing – indeed it will not be able to avert the downward trend of the country's currency in comparison with the major currencies!"

"What evidence do you have to support your claim?" I asked.

"What evidence do you need, my friend? It is an obvious fact! They have their own way of manipulating the market!"

"How?"

"Well, if you are not convinced and need further details, I am happy to meet you at the 'Life is War Chop Bar' (a fast food restaurant) at the far end of this street at an appropriate time. We could, over a glass of beer, discuss the matter in detail."

As I write, the proposed meeting has not taken place. We exchanged mobile phone numbers, so I will attempt to contact him next time I am in Ghana.

For now, I will leave his allegations – very serious allegations they surely are – hanging in the air whilst I concentrate on the task I have set myself.

In view of the challenging economic situation I have just touched upon, indeed in view of the hardships facing the proverbial 'common man' on the street of Accra, the capital and elsewhere in the country, one might be inclined to ask me: 'Are you justified in maintaining the original title *THREE CHEERS FOR GHANA* in this second edition? What after all have those facing daily challenges, indeed hardships brought about by the rising cost of living and other factors, have to cheer about in present-day Ghana?'

Instead of answering the question directly, I shall recall a discussion I had not long ago with my doctor friend who happens to hail from one of the former West African countries which, as in the case of Ghana, used to be under the British: "Ach, the British! At the zenith of their glorious days as World Imperial Power, they were virtually everywhere on the globe!" my friend exclaimed. (I will resist the temptation to delve any deeper into this area, for after all it is not the subject matter under discussion.)

For the sake of discretion, I shall not mention the name of the West African country from which my friend hails. But just by way of a hint I'll say this: it is a country well blessed with Petrodollars! Whether the wealth is being used to advance the lot of the common man (and woman!) on the street is another issue!

My doctor friend in question revealed to me during our conversation that he had not only sent his son to medical school in Ghana, but was considering purchasing a home in Ghana and then move to settle permanently in Ghana.

"You really want to settle in Ghana?" I asked.

"Indeed, yes!"

"Why?"

"I like the place; it is a really peaceful country."

"Well, strangers to Ghana generally speak favourably of the country. However it appears crime is on the increase these days, at least based on what I have read and heard."

"Those concerned about crime in your country should visit my country! Take it from me, I felt very safe when I was walking on the streets of Accra – the situation there is very different from what pertains in my country!"

I am happy that statement did not come from me, so I cannot be accused of bias or of spreading '*fake news*'!

Indeed, despite the economic challenges, Ghana remains a reasonably safe and peaceful place to live.

Not only is the little country on the West African Coast enjoying political stability, it is also a generally free and tolerant society.

Women, for example, are free to do whatever they choose to do within the confines of the law. I will cite a few examples to substantiate my point: The chairperson of the influential Electoral Commission is female; the Chief Justice is female; within the realm of decency a woman can put on anything she wishes without the threat of intimidation from any quarters.

There is also religious tolerance in Ghana: Atheists, Christians, Pagans, Muslims, all live peacefully side by side.

There is also freedom of the press in Ghana. Talking of the freedom of speech and the freedom to publish in today's Ghana, one can in fact publish, broadcast, even propagate whatever one wishes within the confines of the law without fear of persecution from any quarters.

The press in present-day Ghana is so free that it will surely beat that prevailing in several countries in Europe – North, South, East and West!

Indeed, the press in Ghana is freer than the press of some of the well-established western democracies, for it can surely report uncomfortable news about our President without being accused of spreading 'fake news' just because the news they carry does not suit our President.

To substantiate my claim, I visited the website of Reporters Without Borders (https://rsf.org/en/ranking), to seek objective proof of my contention.

And lo and behold, I did not have to search long for proof of my claim, for Ghana I found ranks 26th on the Reporters Without Borders

2017 Press Freedom Ranking, in a total of 180 countries. In other words, only 25 countries out of a list of 180 boast a freer press than Ghana.

I was pleasantly surprised to learn that Ghana was placed far ahead of countries the likes of France (39), the UK (40) and – I could hardly believe my eyes! – the USA (42)!

I do not want to be considered a mouthpiece for the Ministry of Tourism of Ghana, but for anyone wishing to visit my land of birth, I can only state that it is a fairly safe place to visit. I am not implying that it a paradise on earth, a crime-free enclave in an imperfect world free of pick-pockets, fraudsters, robbers, armed and unarmed.

Still, it is safe to say that, aside from the normal risks that can accompany anyone anywhere in the world, it *is* a fairly low-risk country to visit.

Thus, if only for the factors just touched upon – political stability, freedom of the press, general respect for human rights – I will still shout out *THREE CHEERS FOR GHANA!* – irrespective of the economic challenges.

Robert Peprah-Gyamfi
Loughborough, Leicestershire
UK
July 7, 2017

Preface

In these days of the global village, it is not difficult to glean information about Ghana, that relatively small West African state that led black Africa to political independence, and which, as the author of this book puts it, is bravely marching forward with the front-runners for political freedom and economic development on the African continent. Information on the country—its geographical location, its period of political instability, and its phenomenal economical growth—can easily be gleaned from the Internet and various socio-political treatises. Armed with such information, one might assume that anyone visiting the country will be in a better position to understand its history, its politics, its economy and its peoples. But would they, really? I would venture to suggest that reading this book by Dr Robert Peprah-Gyamfi will place one in a much better and stronger position to understand the country and its peoples than any amount of Internet surfing or studying of textbooks will achieve. This is because the writer writes as a partisan, from personal experience and observation, having been born in the country, having grown up there, and having returned there, in the last instance, after thirteen years of absence.

Through the writer we are seeing Ghana constantly from two perspectives— through the eyes of the writer (his memories) before he left (or on his earlier visit) and through the eyes of the Europeanised doctor who returns after thirteen years, who registers his surprise at the changes, for better or for worse, that he sees. As he observes in his Introduction, when he last visited his native Ghana in October, 1994, the country might still have been seen as belonging to the "third-world", whereas in his recent visit, in July 2007, the so-called third world and

xix

the modern industrialised, urbanised, developed world might be seen as existing cheek-by-jowl with each other! Thus on the streets of Accra might be seen women in traditional dress with babies tied to their backs, and smartly dressed "westernised" women driving expensive luxury limousines. Executive mansions might flourish in an affluent area where, however, the new development has outstripped the provision of services, where the roads are muddy and full of potholes.

What makes this book on modern Ghana so accessible, however, is the author's dramatisation of his visit. The reader is, in effect, a fellow traveller with him and his family. We share the excitement of leaving the UK with the family, the packing of the luggage, the impending disappointment and panic when it seems their flight has been cancelled, as well as the sense of adventure when they have to rush to be in time for an alternative flight.

In all the confusion and uncertainty at the outset of the journey, one person, the author says, was prominent on his mind, namely his youngest child Jonathan, and we share with him the urgent hope that the young boy will not be disappointed by a cancelled flight! This very readable book takes us on an entertaining journey, since, in a sense, it reads like a novel—one flies out to Ghana with the author and his family and shares his son's excitement of flying, and so it goes on; this is not a dry treatise on the economic, social and political conditions of Ghana, but a journey in which one meets the people, wonders at the signs of new affluence in the posh houses and expensive German cars driven by sophisticated housewives, travels with the author and his family to their old hometowns, shares the glee of their extended families in seeing them again, gains a personal and moving perspective into the recent past of the indigenous cultures, the poorer farming folk who in some cases still struggle to survive; it is an account of first-hand experience whereby one understands the author's concern to help advance the prospects, not only of the disadvantaged members of the family, but of the country as a whole.

Charles Muller
MA (Wales), Ph.D. (London), D.Litt (OFS), D.Ed (SA)
Diadem Books
www.diadembooks.com

Acknowledgements

O n behalf of Rita my wife and our children Karen, David and Jonathan, I thank God Almighty for taking us safely to Ghana and bringing us back to the UK. I am also indebted to my trusted editor, Dr Charles Muller, proprietor of Diadem Books (www.diadembooks. co.uk) for his marvellous editorial work that gave the manuscript its final glorious finish.

Finally, I am deeply grateful to Mr Francis Akoto, Webmaster of www.ghanaweb.com for his permission to quote the three news items found at the beginning of the book.

Introduction

When I last visited my native Ghana in October, 1994, the country could safely be classified as a third world nation (though I personally detest the idea of classifying countries in this way, based on their respective levels of development). During my recent visit in July 2007, almost thirteen years on, the classification was no longer clear-cut.

As I drove through the city of Accra during the first few days of my stay, it appeared to me as though the first and third worlds had literally crashed together on the streets of the nation's capital; the fallout from the unusual collision was everywhere apparent!

On the congested streets of the city the latest brands of highly valued vehicles— Mercedes, BMW, Jaguar—could be seen driving cheek by jowl with ageing ones, some of which might well be described as death-traps. The roads they jostled on ranged from newly constructed world-class three-lane dual-carriage thoroughfares right down to untarred tracks, some of which had turned muddy and were almost impassable after a downpour of rain.

While some of the areas of the city associated with people of the lower income bracket—Nima, James Town, Pig Farm, etc—had not changed significantly over the years, elsewhere in the city and especially the surrounding suburbs of East Legon, East Airport, Adenta, etc., affluence was very apparent, for these areas had become residential estates boasting luxurious stylish mansions, adorned in some cases by palm-lined boulevards and beautiful front gardens that had sprung up in the recent past to add flair to the scenery. Some of the highly valued properties, showcases of architectural excellence, compare favourably with their counterparts in Malibu, Beverly Hills, and West London.

The traditional image of the African woman is that of an illiterate and deprived individual who is expected to submit to the whims and caprices of her domineering husband and who is condemned in the main to a life of child-bearing and child-rearing. One might have expected many examples of this stereotype in the streets of Accra, but I was confronted with a very different picture in several areas of the city as I observed a not insignificant number of elegantly dressed ladies, some of whose faces radiated a considerable degree of self-confidence; I caught glimpses of such elegant ladies, for instance, behind the wheels of their cars, marques often of the noble class.

Indeed, my native country has made significant strides in her development since my last visit in 1994. A period of political stability coupled with a radical economic restructuring , the Structural Adjustment Programme (SAP), has led to a significant economic turnaround. *Three Cheers for Ghana*, while narrating the personal experience of myself and that of my wife Rita and our three children during our visit to our native Ghana in the summer of 2007, will attempt to describe from our own perspective, the phenomenal economic and structural transformation that have taken place in that country in recent times. While highlighting the positive, the book will not be silent in regard to the negative aspect of the remarkable development. The hope of gaining employment in the capital, for example, has led to a dramatic increase of the population, especially as a result of the massive influx of the youth from the countryside into Accra. That in turn has led to a shortage of accommodation, overcrowding, overburdening of sanitary facilities, increase in crime, etc. Generally, however, Ghana' s success story is worthy of broadcasting, to serve as an example for other developing countries elsewhere in the world.

CHAPTER 1
Plans Derailed at the Eleventh Hour

꒰ᯓ꒱

Lufthansa suspends flights from Accra
A ccra, July 15, GNA—Lufthansa German Airlines says it has been forced to suspend its operations between Accra and Frankfurt following the expiration of its approval for daily flights between the two cities on Saturday July 14, 2007. Briefing the Ghana News Agency in Accra, Ms. Babette Melling, Marketing Manager of Lufthansa, said the airline was informed by the Ghanaian Ministry of Aviation that government approval for the airline's daily flights to Ghana had expired and it would be allowed only two flights a week connecting Accra with Frankfurt.

Unfortunately, however, the airline cannot accept the option of two flights a week, since this is not an economically viable proposition. Lufthansa truly regrets being forced to take Ghana off its destination map from 15th July under these circumstances.

She explained that the last flight, LH 565, departed on Saturday, 14th July, from Accra to Frankfurt (via Lagos) arriving in Frankfurt on Sunday morning. Ms Melling said Lufthansa and Ghana have enjoyed a long and dedicated commitment of 40 years and are happy for the collaboration. The flight connections to Lagos/Nigeria remain unaffected

I could hardly believe my eyes concerning what I was reading! Lufthansa no longer flies to Ghana! No, that cannot be true—it must be a bad joke! I turned over to the Lufthansa homepage to find out whether I could find a confirmation of what I had just read. No, there was nothing to that effect. The only thing that provided some clue was the fact that Accra was no longer present on the list of destination Airports to which the airline was flying.

Next, I consulted Google. I typed in 'Lufthansa no longer flying to Accra' and began the search. As I glanced through the results, I came across the account of someone who was due to fly with the airline from the US to Ghana a few days before. According to him he went to the airport only to be told he could not fly with that airline. After much protest at the Lufthansa counter, followed by several telephone calls by the staff, he was finally put on a different airline.

As the bitter reality began to sink in, I grew increasingly nervous. I looked at the clock on the wall, which told me it was 01:35 hrs on Tuesday, 17th July 2007. At that time of day, one would expect me to be in deep sleep in my bed, probably snoring (as my other half says I am frequently accustomed to do) and lost in a dream only God knows what about. Nothing of the sort! I was neither enjoying the comfort of my bed, nor was I disturbing the sleep of other members of the family with my loud snores. Where was I, then?

Well, I was seated behind a large computer desk in a hall measuring about 30 metres in length and 30 metres in breadth. Surrounding me on each side were several other computer desks, each equipped with a computer as well as a telephone fitted with a recording device. I was not alone in the hall; two other individuals, a lady aged about thirty as well as a gentleman of about twenty, were my companions. The setting was in Leicester, a city located in the English Midlands about 160 Kilometres to the north of London.

What was keeping me awake at that time of the night? To be honest, it was primarily money. Yes, the need to earn a living to provide not only for my nuclear family and meet various personal financial commitments, but also to assist members of my extended family in Ghana had led me to sacrifice my sleep. Then, also, was the desire on my part to apply the knowledge I had acquired over the years in the area of medical science to help bring a cure to others. In short—I was doing an overnight session in my duty as a General Practitioner.

'In that unusual setting?' one might ask. Yes, indeed. I was doing telephone consulting, performing what is known in the medical practice of the UK and some other countries as 'triage'. The term *triage* I understand is borrowed from the French word *tri* which, translated into English, means 'sort'.

Triaging is said to have originally been practised on the battlefield. Faced with several casualties who needed to be attended to by the limited medical personnel, the cases were prioritised, based on the severity of the injuries and the threat they posed to their victims. Attention was subsequently given in order of decreasing severity of injuries.

Triaging is widely practised in UK primary medical care. Usually the calls of patients seeking medical help or advice are first received by call handlers. They in turn take down the details of callers and the reasons for the calls. The cases are then passed on to the duty doctor or nurse. The calls so passed appear a few seconds later on the screens of the doctor or nurse as the case may be.

The nurse or doctor handling a case basically has three options—to provide advice on the phone, to ask the caller to travel to a Primary Care Centre (PCC) for a face-to-face consultation with a doctor, or where the condition of the patient so demands it, either send an emergency ambulance to provide urgent care or else despatch a doctor to a routine home visit.

Owing to the volume of work during the daytime and also during the early hours of the night several telephonists, nurses and doctors are usually involved in the triage process during that period. Towards midnight and thereafter staff is reduced considerably. In our case the staff was reduced to a doctor and two call handlers after midnight.

The overnight session I was working began from 23:59 hrs till 08:00 hrs the following morning. One may well puzzle over the timing 23:59 hrs. Initially I was also baffled. As it later dawned on me, the timing is so designed to assign the date of work to the previous day, just before it breaks into a new one. Thus the beginning of the particular session I am referring to was 23:59 hrs on Monday 16th.

As to be expected, the workload of a particular session is unpredictable. On some nights the calls came in very sparingly; on other nights one was literally overwhelmed by the number of those seeking medical help at that time of night, a fact that sometimes led me to wonder whether the whole population of the county had decided to stay awake!

The call for medical advice or help could come from patients (or their relatives, as the case maybe) for various reasons—ranging from patients with life-threatening conditions such as heart attacks, strokes, severe breathing problems, to those considering taking their lives right down to those seeking advice about what to do next after accidentally swallowing the medication meant for the next morning just as they were about to retire to bed!

Compassion, patience, tact and the ability to relate to others are required of the doctor on the phone, not only on account of his or her desire to uphold the integrity of the profession but also in his/her personal interest, for the average patient in the British Isles is not known to shun the path of written complaints.

Even should such complaints turn out to be baseless, one still has to respond to them. To avoid having to spend precious time behind a writing desk thinking of how best to formulate a response appropriate to a particular complaint, one is best advised to go to all possible lengths at the outset to ward off a complaint.

Admittedly, it is easier said than done. During a face-to-face consultation, one has the advantage of visual contact, helping one to come to terms with an aggrieved patient who needs to be appeased. That is not always the case on the phone.

The workload on the night in question was not particularly heavy. After a relatively busy start matters soon eased considerably.

As was my custom on such nights, I decided to while away the time by way of the Internet. After visiting several online medical journals, I turned to the online editions of some of the world's leading news organizations to keep myself abreast with the happenings of our world.

From time to time I returned to the operational programme to ascertain whether a case had in the meantime come in. I

In the course of Internet surfing I decided to visit Ghanaweb.com, one of the leading sites on matters relating to Ghana. I had made it a habit to visit the site at least once daily to keep abreast with events at home. First I glanced through the headlines for Monday 16th July. One particular headline caught my attention:

4

Nigerians arrested with fake new cedi notes.

I clicked on it to read the whole story:

Aflao, July 16, GNA—Two Nigerians were arrested on Saturday by Customs officials at the Aflao border for possessing fake new Ghana cedi notes. The watermark and the silver lining, the two main security features of the new Ghana cedi note, were not on the notes found on them. The suspects—Michael Akinniyi Adetayo, 35, and 36-year-old Sunday Olaole Ogundeyi, have since been handed over to the Aflao police for further investigation.

Mr Ahmed Issah Yakubu, Assistant Superintendent of Police in charge of Aflao district, told the Ghana News Agency that the two Nigerians arrived at the last departure checkpoint at about 0630 hours on Saturday.

He said Customs officers, who had been on the alert for fake notes, examined the two thoroughly and found the fake currency in GHC1 and GHC10 denominations. Mr Yakubu said the two claimed the notes were given to them when they went to exchange Naira into cedis while on their way to shop in Accra. The Police have impounded their luggage.

Mr Yakubu said the two would be brought before court on Tuesday for conspiracy and possessing fake notes.

Source GNA

Imagine that—managing to falsify currency notes that had been in circulation for barely fourteen days! The two must be smart cheats indeed, I said to myself! It was still quiet on the 'work front' so I decided to read through other headlines from the recent past. In the process, I returned to the headlines from July 15th—

British girls 'knew they were coming to Ghana to smuggle drugs'

This was too compelling to skip so I clicked on it:

London (UK Independent)—British officials in Ghana were yesterday trying to ensure the two British schoolgirls arrested trying to leave the country with £300,000 worth of cocaine hidden in laptop bags are moved to "more appropriate" juvenile detention accommodation before their first court date on Wednesday. Yasemin Vatansever and Yatunde Diya, from north London, were moved on Friday to the headquarters of the narcotics control board where they are sharing a cell. They face 10 years in prison if found guilty.

A senior narcotics officer who interrogated the girls following their arrest as they tried to board a flight to London described the moment they were caught. "They were carrying their luggage to the airport departure formalities when the operations saw they had a laptop bag," he told the BBC. "When they opened it, it was empty but when they lifted it, it was heavy. They cut it and saw there was a white substance. It was proved to be cocaine." He added: "They knew what they were coming to do in Ghana. They were asked by a certain Ghanaian, by the name of Jay, to come to Ghana and pick up two laptop bags for a fee of £3,000."

Campaign group Fair Trials Abroad has raised concerns about the girls' treatment. They were arrested on 2nd July and questioned without lawyers present. They also say that as the girls are minors they should have been allowed to fly to London before being arrested. The group is now ensuring the girls have proper legal support.

The case highlights a new front in the so-called war on drugs. This has seen South America's drug lords doing multimillion-pound business with West Africa's military and political leaders. Routes for bringing cocaine into Britain and Europe have changed in the past few months with West Africa becoming the major transit point between Colombia and Europe. Up to 20 "mules", or drug couriers, a week are believed to be arriving in Britain from the region.

The British girls were stopped by Ghanaian Narcotic Control Board officers, who are part of Operation Westbridge, a project set up by HM Revenue and Customs and the Ghanaian authorities. An HMRC spokesman said: "Operation Westbridge has been going since November, and has already stopped £10m worth of drugs heading to the UK and Europe. These girls are not the first British nationals to be arrested but they are the youngest." Source: GHP

As might be expected the case of the two teenagers made headline news in the UK and generated considerable public interest and debate. A few days earlier I had listened to a report on BBC Radio 5. The speaker, while not being against the arrest as such, was of the opinion that, considering their age, the Ghanaian authorities should have allowed them to fly out of the country in order to be arrested on their arrival at Heathrow. Among other things, she based her reasoning on the poor conditions of the prisons in Ghana as well as problems of communication. When the presenter pointed out to her that Ghana was a former British colony where English was still the official language, she countered with the words that the arrested girls might not understand the way Ghanaians speak their English!

Her comments called to my mind the saying: 'Whatever you do, people will talk about you!' It has lately been reported in several quarters in the West that the drug bosses in South America are increasingly using the West African sub-region as transit points for onward trafficking of cocaine to the Western World. Accusing fingers in the West have been pointing to governments in the West African sub-region for not doing enough to curtail the illicit trafficking.

As long as other nationals are arrested, all is fine. Now that their own nationals have been caught in the act they seem to have panicked. Will they be able to keep their nerve and ensure that justice takes its course?

Concerning the term 'more appropriate', I read between the lines and understood what the British official was driving at. Over the last several months, I have been engaged as locum GP in one of Her Majesty's Prisons. I have in the process gained some insight into the conditions pertaining in such prisons.

The living conditions of the prisoners there cannot in any way be described as 'not appropriate' or 'inappropriate'. Apart from regular meals, the quality of which cannot be described as bad, the inmates have access to adequate medical and dental care. Inmates who do not have the means to pay their legal bills have access to solicitors paid by the state. Social workers frequent the prisons to help inmates sort out issues pertaining to the family, work, accommodation, etc. Inmates who are in a position to work are offered jobs that attract wages.

To while away their time and also to keep fit, inmates can choose to visit a well-equipped Gym, engage in outdoor games such as football, visit the library, watch TV, etc.

Is it surprising that some of them, especially those addicted to drugs and who claim to have no fixed addresses in the free world, fall into depression at the thought of being released? Some have confided in me that they intentionally re-offend on their release in order to be sent back 'home'.

Although I had not been in Ghana for almost thirteen years and could not claim to know the exact conditions under which prisoners there were kept at the time in question, it was still obvious to me that it would in no way match those just described.

I was about to leave the Internet and turn my attention to something else, when something urged me to take a final glance through the headlines of Sunday July 15th. Then it happened! My eyes chanced upon the headline towards the very bottom of the list: ***Lufthansa no longer flying to Ghana.*** With a nervous hand, I clicked on it to read the unsettling story.

Lufthansa, the Airline my whole family—Rita and myself as well as our children, Karen, David and Jonathan—was scheduled to fly on the following day, was no longer flying to the very destination we were heading for! And no one had informed us to that effect!

We were scheduled to depart from Birmingham International Airport at 06:50 hrs the next morning, 18th July. After a short stopover at the Frankfurt International Airport we were to resume our journey at 11:30 hrs and finally touch down at the Accra International Airport at 17:20 hrs.

The journey home had been planned several months ahead, culminating in the final booking at the beginning of April. The decision to fly with the German carrier was not taken spontaneously but after careful consideration.

Naturally we preferred a direct flight from the UK to Ghana. After searching on the Internet for a while, I realised there were only two airlines offering such flights—British Airways (BA) and Ghana International Airline (GIA). It has been my tendency to patronise everything 'Made in Ghana.' In line with that I flew with the state-owned Ghana Airways during my visits home in 1988, 1991 and 1994.

For reasons that in my judgement cannot include lack of patronage of the Airline by the large Ghanaian community in Europe and North America, the Airline went bust in 2004.

The GIA was set up in 2004 as a partnership between the Ghana government and a group of private international investors to pick up where the state carrier gave up. For reasons that I do not want to enumerate here, I decided, at least for that particular trip, to avoid it.

We decided against BA on the grounds of economics—flying that airline would have cost us about £1000 above what we would need to pay to fly with another airlines with a comparable reputation.

Having eliminated the two direct flights, we were left with about half a dozen others with transit stops in various airports in Africa and Europe to choose from. After eliminating the others for various reasons we were left with KLM and Lufthansa, the Dutch and German carriers respectively, to choose between.

The decision to opt for the German carrier was not based on monetary considerations (the fare offered by both airlines was almost identical) but rather on the transit time.

David, our second child, displays the autistic trait and has difficulty adjusting to change, in particular that involving having to be with several strangers in an enclosed place. For this reason we chose a transit time that would be as brief as possible. Flying KLM would have required a longer waiting time in Amsterdam compared to the time we would spend at Frankfurt.

Or did our long association with Germany affect our decision for Lufthansa? Indeed, before we settled in the UK in February 2006, we lived in Germany. I for one had lived almost uninterruptedly there since 1982. The fact that I was able to train to become a doctor was largely a result of the German Development Program that offered a percentage of university admissions to students from developing countries. It was in Germany, namely at the main train station in Hannover, that Rita and I first got to know each other, and it was in that northern German city that all our three children were born.

Lufthansa no longer flying to Accra! My first thought was to try and contact the airline. Although I guessed no one would respond to the call at that time of day—or night—I nevertheless decided to give it a try. Soon I was back on the homepage. After noting down their hotline, I left for the staff rest room adjacent the main hall. Using my mobile phone, I got through to them.

I was greeted by an automatic answering device. After pressing a few numbers as instructed, I was finally told to wait for an adviser: *Do not hang up—your call is important to us; it will be dealt with as soon as possible by the next available staff member*. This recorded message was repeated again and again. I waited dutifully as the time ticked away. After waiting several minutes without any sign of the promised adviser I ended the call and returned to the hall, anxiety mingled with frustration written on my face.

In the meantime, a couple of cases had cropped up on the screen. It took me about twenty minutes to deal with them. Shortly afterwards I was back in the rest room. As on the previous occasion, I waited to no avail for someone to speak to. Over the next several minutes, I would try on many occasions to get someone from the airline to speak to— to no avail.

In all the confusion and uncertainty, one person was prominent on my mind, namely Jonathan. Ever since he got to know about the forthcoming visit to Ghana several weeks before, and in particular since the school vacation began five days earlier, his thoughts had largely been occupied by it. Not only the thought of meeting relatives, but the excitement of flying made him yearn for the journey to Africa. Since his first experience with aeroplanes during our visit to South Africa five months earlier, he had grown fond of flying. On that occasion, his disappointment was only too evident when he was not able to occupy a window seat. It goes without saying that this time he was eagerly awaiting a new opportunity for a window seat! His mind was so set on flying the following day that even a day's postponement would surely spell disaster for him! Can you imagine his desolation if we were forced to cancel the holiday altogether?

CHAPTER 2
Rescued by a Virgin

I breathed a sigh of relief as the clock finally turned to register 08:00 hrs. At last, I could leave for home and gear my effort towards averting the impending 'catastrophe'. After about thirty minutes' drive northwards on the M1, the highway that divides England from north to south in approximately two equal halves, I finally approached our home in Loughborough, about twenty kilometres away.

As I drove past the bus stop located about two hundred metres from our home, I saw the rest of the family gathered there. Jonathan waved at me as he spotted my vehicle on the other side of the road. Just as I was wondering what they were waiting for at that time of day, it dawned on me that Karen had an appointment with her hairdresser in Leicester that morning. The poor helpless newborn babe who lay helpless in a cot on the infant ward of a hospital in Hannover fourteen years before had developed into a teenager bubbling with energy! She was desirous of getting her hair in shape just before setting out on the journey to the land of her ancestors.

Though their mother possessed a driving licence and could have waited for my return to use the car, she had been reluctant to drive in the UK. She was not comfortable with driving on the left side of the road contrary to what she was used to in Germany. Partly because I was driving on the far side of the road, partly because the bus was expected to arrive at any moment, and also because I did not want to break the news to them, I merely waved back and drove on.

The first thing I did on getting home was to reach for the phone. Without hesitation, I dialled the Lufthansa hotline one more time. This time, again, an automatic system responded—but on this occasion I was thankfully directed to a human adviser!

I told her what I had read on the Internet—I was scheduled to fly with them to the very destination that had now been discontinued. How best could she help me? She admitted hearing the news for the first time and urged me to hang on whilst she informed herself from appropriate quarters. She was back after a short while.

'Unfortunately, I can only confirm your information,' she began. 'A problem has developed between us and the Ghanaian authorities. This has led them to withdraw landing rights for our airline. Under the circumstances, we are left with no other option than to suspend our flights.'

'What should I do then?' I inquired nervously.

'I will check whether I can re-book you on one of our partner airlines. If you don't mind hanging up now, I will get back to you shortly.'

A few tense minutes followed during which I wavered between hope and despair. Finally she was back.

'I am afraid I do not have any good news for you. As you are aware, this is the peak of the holiday season. I checked with our partner airlines KLM and BA to ascertain whether I could find you seats. Regrettably they are all fully booked. The next available flight will be in about fourteen days from now!'

'What a shame! We booked our flight as far back as April only to be disappointed at the eleventh hour!'

'I am terribly sorry, but there is little I can do. You have two options—either to postpone your flight until such time that we are able to offer you a flight or request a refund.'

On hearing the word *refund*, a feeling of hopelessness mingled with anger and frustration overwhelmed me. Why, for heavens sake, had the problem cropped up at the very last minute?!

Was it out of desperation? Was it on account of refusing to accept reality? Was it for both reasons? Whatever the reason, I decided not to accept the information from Lufthansa in Birmingham as the final word.

Instead I decided to take advantage of my knowledge of the German language to contact the airline directly in Germany.

I might as well have spared myself the time and also the money! In the end the lady I met on the phone could only confirm what her colleague in Birmingham had told me. Her attempt to find us an alternative flight yielded the same negative result.

As I placed the receiver back on the phone my eyes caught sight of the several pieces of luggage scattered in the living room ready for the journey to Africa. We had spent the last several days packing. In the process Rita, who did the greater part of the job, had taken great pains to ensure that we did not exceed the 100 kilograms allocated to the five of us. With the aid of our home digital scale we had conducted an exercise in weighing, discarding items we deemed not absolutely essential for the journey, re-weighing, abandoning still more non-essentials, and once more re-weighing . After we had gone through the process a few times, we realised to our disgust that we were left with forty kilograms of belongings we could not do without. In the end we decided to dispatch them as unaccompanied cargo ahead of us. Accompanied by Jonathan, I had driven the approximately eighty kilometres distance to the Birmingham International Airport the previous day to deliver the overflow luggage to a handling agent. What would happen to it should we be unable to embark on our journey?

Another issue that troubled me was the accommodation we were already booked into in Accra. The rooms had been booked on our behalf several weeks in advance. Although neither Rita nor I hailed from the capital, our intention was to spend the first few days there before moving on to the countryside to visit our respective hometowns. We intended to use the time in the national capital visiting relatives and friends and also showing the children places of interest in the Accra-Tema metropolitan area.

On my previous visits to Ghana, I stayed with Ransford, my brother and his family in their spacious flat in an apartment building in Tema, a town about twenty kilometres to the east of Accra. He has in the meantime moved with his entire family to settle in London. Although they still maintained the flat, we could not use it on this particular occasion because of the refurbishment going on there.

To solve our accommodation problem, I contacted my friend Kwasi, who had in the meantime risen to the position of district medical officer at a district hospital in a town a few kilometres to the north of Kumasi. As on previous occasions when I had sought his help, he was forthcoming as usual, promising to do whatever he could to help.

He did not have to look far for a solution to the problem. His brother-in-law, the brother of Georgina, his wife, runs a hotel in Accra. Attached to the main hotel building is a smaller building boasting two bedrooms and equipped with self-catering facilities. It is meant for a family like ours who needed it for a short stay. We asked him to book us into the facility for the first fourteen days of our stay. How would his brother-in-law react should we decide to cancel the booking at the last minute? Would we be made to pay compensation?

The clock on the wall in the living room meanwhile read 09:30 hrs. Just then an idea occurred to me—to contact the travel agency where I did the booking. Maybe they could find us some last-minute seats on another airline! Moments later I was heading for the centre of town. Before long I was knocking on their door.

Just as on my two previous encounters with Lufthansa, the sales agent I spoke to was also hearing my story for the first time. They could also not find us any seats at such short notice for, as it turned out, they dealt with only the well-established airlines, all of which were fully booked at that time of year.

For the first time since the drama began to evolve I began seriously to consider possible alternatives to the Ghana trip. For the sake of the children, in particular Jonathan, we would need to travel somewhere, at any rate. How would we otherwise manage to keep them occupied throughout the six-week holiday? Possible destinations could be South Africa (which had fascinated us during our stay in February), or Holland to visit Thomas, my brother, or Germany, to visit various friends. Still, I was determined not to give up; at least not without a fight. The time, meanwhile, was a few minutes past ten.

I decided as a last resort to check the Internet for a possible last-minute flight to Ghana. I decided not to lose precious time driving home for that purpose, but rather make use of an Internet cafe a stone's throw away. Soon I found myself navigating through the virtual milieu of the

World Wide Web. My first stop was Google. Nervously I typed the words *last minute flights to Accra Ghana* into the search engine. Moments later several related sites appeared on the screen.

Initially I selected three of them, including the Ghana International that I had originally decided to avoid. On this occasion, I decided to try them first. On dialling their number, I was greeted by a male adviser, who, judging from his accent, I assumed was a Ghanaian.

'I am desperately looking for seats for a family of five, two adults and three children, on your London-Accra flight.' Thus I began after the initial greetings.

'When do you intend flying, sir?'

'As soon as possible; preferably tomorrow.'

'How old are the children?'

'14, 10 and 6 years.'

'We classify the 14-year-old as an adult, sir.'

'Okay; seats for three adults and two children, please.'

'Did I hear you say that you are prepared to fly tomorrow?'

'That is correct!'

'Yes indeed, I can offer you five seats on tomorrow's flight.'

'It is just splendid!'

'They are first class seats, however.'

'We want to fly economy, please.'

'Unfortunately that is fully booked.'

'No seats in the economy-class!' I repeated. Had I heard him correctly?

'That is exactly the case, sir.'

'How much do they cost?'

'Approximately £800 for Adults and £600 for children, adding up to about £7200 for the round tickets for all of you.'

'No discounts?'

'No sir!'

Despite the burning desire to travel home, I knew the fare was a non-starter, for it would stretch our resources to the very limit—for although Lufthansa was talking of a refund, it would take some time for the money to reach my account. Under the circumstances, I decided to adopt a strategy that I thought might help—to plead with him in the Twi language spoken by the majority in Ghana.

'Please, do us a favour and permit us to pay economy prices for the available seats,' I began in Twi.

He was indeed at home with the language for he replied in the same language.

'No, that cannot be done,' he insisted.

'Please help; after all, you will be flying tomorrow: I doubt very much that you will manage to fill the seats by then.'

'No, that is not possible,' he refused to budge.

'Okay, give me some time to think over your proposal; you will hear from me again should I decide to accept it.'

Next I dialled the second number on the list. I was greeted by a male voice. Without any waste of time, I made the reason for my call known to him. On hearing what I had to say, he asked me to give him some time while he checked his computer. Moments later his voice filled the receiver.

'I could place you on a Lufthansa flight from Birmingham to Lagos, scheduled for tomorrow. When you get to Lagos you will easily find a flight to Accra.'

I rejected his offer without much consideration. It would almost certainly mean having to hang around at the airport with the several pieces of luggage we were carrying, looking for a flight to our final destination. No, not in Lagos, of all places, I said to myself.

'No other possibilities?' I inquired, almost at the point of giving up all hope of flying home any time soon.

'Please spare me a few more minutes. I have to consult our system again.'

In the background I could hear the sounds emanating from his fingers typing on the keyboard of his computer.

He was back a few minutes later with a question I had least expected.

'Are you prepared to fly tonight, sir?'

'Tonight?' I inquired, more out of surprise than not having heard him well.

'Yes indeed! I am able to put all of you on a flight tonight. You will not be flying from Birmingham, but from London Gatwick. You will have to make a short transit in Lagos, however.'

'A transit in Lagos?'

'Yes.'

'Which airline is that?'

'Virgin Nigeria.'

'Virgin Nigeria?'

'Yes indeed; departure time is 23:00 hrs'

I was so taken aback by the sudden turn of events that for a moment I was at a loss to know how to react to his offer. I began to think. I had read in the news about the arrangement between Virgin Airlines and the Nigerian government to operate in that country. I reasoned that as far as the fleet of airplanes was concerned, they would reflect the high standards associated with the mother airline. Since according to him the transit time in Lagos would be short, it should not be a problem for David. The only problem I envisaged was the short time at our disposal.

A look at my watch told me it was in the meanwhile 10:45 hrs. Not only did we ourselves have to get ready for the journey, we needed to drive a distance of approximately 270 kilometres to the airport.

'Are you prepared to accept the offer?' he asked after a while.

'How much will it cost us?'

'Two adults and three children, you said?'

'Yes, three children aged 14, 10 and 6 years.'

'The 14-year-old counts as an adult.'

'Okay, three adults and two children!'

'Please bear with me while I calculate.'

A short silence followed.

'Altogether, £3400 for the return journey.'

That meant £400 above the price of the original flight. Never mind, I said to myself. Fortunately, I still had enough funds in my accounts to cover it.

'Okay, go ahead and book it!'

CHAPTER 3
Styling for Africa

F rom there I drove straight home; the rest of the family were yet to arrive. I dialled our second mobile number to pass the latest news to them—and to my dismay I realised the phone had been switched off! It also occurred to me that I did not have the number of the hairdresser's shop.

What should be done? Drive to the stylist shop and pick them up? What if they happened to have left by the time I got there? In the end I resolved to wait a while and hope for their early return.

Finally, at around 13:00 hrs I breathed a sigh of relief when I heard the lock to the main door of our home turn. My joy was short-lived for Karen was not in the group.

'Where have you left her?' I inquired in exasperation.

'At the hairdressers,' her unsuspecting mother began. 'We left her there a while ago to purchase a few items still needed for the journey. The stylist expects to be done with her by 14:00 hrs. They will call us when they are about to complete so that she can be picked up.'

'I have to pick her up immediately!'

'Why the rush?'

'Get ready everyone, we are flying *tonight*!' I said emphatically.

'That must be a joke!'

'I thought we are flying tomorrow, Papa?' Jonathan inquired.

'No, we are flying tonight!'

'Why?' her mother inquired.

'Lufthansa is no longer flying to Ghana, at least for the time being.'

'That cannot be true!'

'Yes it is! I have managed to organise another flight. We are flying tonight with Virgin Nigeria.'

'Virgin Nigeria?'

'Yes, from London Gatwick to Lagos, and then Accra!'

'From *London*!'

'Yes! We need to hurry.'

'Why is Lufthansa no longer flying to Ghana?'

'They say they have problems with their landing rights. I think it has got to do with money; it looks as if Ghana is demanding additional money for those rights; they seem unwilling to pay. That has led to the stand-off.'

'Ghana standing up to Germany!'

'David versus Goliath, you might call it!'

'So now we, the passengers who have nothing to do with the matter, have to suffer?'

'Well, that is what it boils down to. Anyway! You get everyone ready. I will hurry to pick up Karen. We must leave for the airport as soon as possible, latest by 17:00 hrs.'

Seconds later I was out of the house. After about half an hour's drive, I pulled up in front of the hairstylist's shop. It was located in an area of the city I do my best to avoid owing to difficulty in finding a parking space. As I had anticipated, all parking spaces were occupied on my arrival.

What was to be done? I noticed a construction site a few metres ahead of me. I discovered a small space separating it from the pavement, meant for pedestrians. I managed to manoeuvre my vehicle into it.

A short while later I stepped into the shop. I had been there on a few occasions to pick her up so my face was not unfamiliar. Even before I could utter a word, one of the ladies approached me, a broad smile on her face.

'Please give us ten more minutes, sir. We are putting finishing touches to it. We want to turn her into a lovely African princess.'

I nodded my approval without uttering a word. Soon I was back in my car. I switched on my radio to BBC World Service to follow the latest events in the world. No sooner had I taken my seat than I spotted in the driving mirror a traffic warden about fifty metres away, heading in my direction!

'I will escape you before you get me!' I said to myself. Seconds later I was speeding away.

For once I had escaped those obnoxious agents of the powers that be—the traffic wardens of the cities of this world! Whilst in Germany, I was irritated by their antics. Since my arrival in the UK I had come to realise, as someone put it, that *nowhere is safe!* The tactics they apply, particularly in the British capital, makes one wonder whether indeed they are there to regulate parking in the city, or whether they harbour ulterior motives, in particular the need to balance the books of the city's administration.

The other day I read the story of someone who was involved in an accident in London whilst driving on his motorbike. As he lay on the street in agony, a traffic warden came by. Instead of offering assistance to the injured, he handed him a ticket for parking his motorbike wrongly on the street!

This once, however, I had managed to escape the law enforcing agents. After driving aimlessly around the congested streets of central Leicester for about ten minutes, I returned. There was still no available space to park the vehicle. The space where I had parked earlier was still vacant, however. After convincing myself that a street warden was nowhere to be seen I parked there once again. Soon I was back in the salon. Karen was no longer in the spot where I found her previously. I took a second look around the large room. *There* she was, in one corner, seated behind a washbasin. Behind her stood one of the stylists, still busily occupied with her hair!

'Give us a few minutes, we are getting her in good shape for Africa!' said the lady who had spoken to me earlier, a broad smile on her face.

These ladies definitely had no idea how hard-pressed we were with time. I had to make the situation clear to them without any further delay, I thought.

'For goodness sake, please release this girl to me,' I said. 'We are flying tonight; we need to hurry to catch our flight in London.'

'Tonight!' Karen shouted in disbelief.

'Yes indeed, we have got to fly tonight.'

'I thought we were flying tomorrow.'

'No, things have changed in a dramatic fashion; we must fly tonight.'

On hearing that all activity on her hair was stopped forthwith.

'Indeed, I was just finishing,' the stylist said. 'I just wanted to do some polishing, to make it look more appealing.'

'Thank you very much for your service; her mother will take care of the rest.'

Her words, 'Have a safe journey to Africa!' followed us from the hall as we stepped outside.

'Thank you very much!' I shouted back.

We got home without any incident. Rita had used the time to get everything ready for the journey.

I still needed to get a few important things done. Most important of all, I needed to despatch an e-mail to Kwasi in Ghana. Based on the original travel schedule, he had organised for someone to pick us up from the airport in the evening of the next day. I had to let him know of our new arrival time, which was scheduled for 09:00 hrs the next day. As a double security I needed to call my niece Joyce to instruct her to organise a second vehicle to meet us on arrival.

Finally I had to call on Dieter, our neighbour, to hand him our keys. He had agreed to play the role of caretaker in our absence. He expected us to travel the next day. He was surprised when he opened his door and heard what I had to tell him.

It was a few minutes past 17:00 hrs when we finally set out on our journey to the airport. Anyone who has driven through England, particularly Southern England, will bear me out concerning the frequent congestions on the highways. As we set out, our prayer was that we would be spared any significant congestion that could lead to a notable delay on the motorway. Heaven heard our prayers, for though the radio in the vehicle announced congestions and delays around London, our route was not affected.

It was about 20:00 hrs when we pulled up in the parking lot a few kilometres away from the airport where I had booked to park my vehicle during our absence. The final few kilometres to the Airport was covered by way of shuttle bus operated by the parking company.

The lady at the check-in desk was surprised that, contrary to the majority of the passengers on the flight, we checked in luggage weighing just about half the maximum allowance. As it turned out, the airline permitted 46 kg per passenger instead of the usual 20kg for that particular flight. The realisation that I might as well have spared the journey to Birmingham made me more than a little furious.

Finally, at around 23:20 hrs, after a few minutes' delay, the powerful engines of the aircraft lifted the huge man-made bird, packed almost to the last seat with souls heading for various destinations, into the dark, near midnight skies over London.

As we ascended high, high above the earth's surface, it occurred to me that I had been awake for over twenty-four hours. I looked forward first to the meals, then hopefully to a smooth flight that would permit some sleep to revive my exhausted body.

CHAPTER 4
Lena's Inn

W e landed on schedule at the Murtala Mohammed Airport in Lagos. Due to the short time at our disposal, we had not been able to obtain a transit visa. This however did not become an issue. The airline was aware of the passengers on transit to Ghana and assisted us at the immigration desk.

After spending about an hour in the transit lounge, we were called upon to proceed to board the Virgin Nigeria flight heading for Accra. A short while later we were airborne. The flight was scheduled to last about forty-five minutes.

From time to time, I took a look at my watch to figure out how long I still needed to wait till touchdown. Wasn't it strange on my part to behave in that way, having waited almost thirteen years for the occasion?

In view of the long period that had elapsed since my last visit one is bound to ask why it took me that long to visit home, considering the fact that Ghana and Europe are not that far apart. Indeed, a direct flight from Amsterdam, Berlin or London lasts hardly seven hours. On frequent occasions in the past I have asked myself the same question. Indeed, at the time I left Accra, in October 1994 after a three-week stay in Ghana on the occasion of my mother's parting from this life, little did I imagine that it would take me this long to return. Man proposes, but God disposes, the saying goes. Owing to several factors regarding my work, the growth of our family, financial constraints, etc., Rita and I had not been able to fulfil the desire in our hearts to be united with our respective families until then.

It was a few minutes past 09:00 hrs when the pilot announced our descent to Accra. A short while later we touched down safely at the Accra International Airport.

It was not the smile of the morning African sun I had expected for a welcome. Instead it was cloudy and raining slightly on touchdown.

The arrival hall had seen a facelift. There were still posters and other memorabilia from the 'Ghana@50' celebrations to mark the 50th anniversary of the country's independence from British colonial rule on 6th March 1957. We needed about twenty minutes to go through immigration. Finally we headed for the outside.

As Karen and I each pushed the two trolleys on which our luggage was piled, a man of about forty wearing the typical bright yellow vest of the airport security approached me and asked:

'May I help you push it?'

'No, thanks,' I replied, 'I can manage it myself.'

'You just allow me to help,' he insisted and began to walk by my side, pushing the trolley from the side as we went. Reluctantly, I left the whole assignment to him. Soon he was pushing it briskly down an alley leading to the main exit. All of a sudden he did something unexpected— he stopped for a short while, pulled off the yellow security vest he wore over his clothes and squeezed it into one of the pockets of his trousers.

'What is he up to?' I asked Rita in a low voice.

'Apparently, he does not want those outside to identify him as belonging to the security,' she reasoned.

Though away from home for a long period of time, I had not forgotten the 'rules of the game'. It was indeed clear to me that such 'kind' gestures are not made for free and that at the end of the day, I would be required to 'do something.'

What was to be done, since we did not have any local currency?

Just as I was considering how I would resolve the problem, he stopped suddenly, about fifty metres from the main exit.

'I do not want to be seen outside the building,' he said. 'It could cost me my job.'

So saying, he handed the trolley over to me and began to look at me with an eager expectancy.

I pulled out my wallet, unzipped it and examined the few notes inside it. My eyes caught sight of a five-pound note. I pulled it out and handed it to him. He took a quick look at it and placed it quickly into his pocket. A broad smile on his face, he thanked us and wished us a happy stay. Soon he was heading back to where he had come from.

His joy was not without reason, for he had received an equivalent of about 10 Ghana cedis, which, with certainty, was far above his daily official earning. Just as I began to push the trolley, a middle-aged man broke loose from the crowd gathered at the main exist waiting to welcome relatives, friends and others and headed towards us.

'Do you need a taxi?' he inquired in a loud voice as he drew near.

'No, someone is coming to pick us up!'

'Bad luck for me! Still, I would like to help push your luggage.'

Even before we could respond he was giving me a helping hand.

'It's okay, I can push it myself,' I protested

'Let me help you, Massa (Mister)!' he persisted and kept on pushing.

As we drew closer to the crowd, a young woman aged about twenty rushed towards us with a smile and outstretched arms, shouting, 'Wofaoooh! Wofaoooh' (Good to see you uncle! Good to see you uncle!)

By virtue of her resemblance to Afia, our youngest sister, I took her to be Joyce and hurried towards her.

How much the little girl of seven I had met during my last visit had changed! Indeed, had it not been for the resemblance to her mother, I would not have recognised the slim, graceful and attractive young woman before me. A period of embracing and shaking of hands with all members of the whole family followed.

Hardly had we gone through the greeting and introduction formalities than the second gentleman who had offered his unsolicited help stretched out his arms towards me.

'Massa, please give me something for my breakfast!' he began.

'But no one requested your help!'

'Massa, have mercy on me, for we are suffering here!'

'Have you got some local currency to spare, Joyce?'

'How much should I give him, uncle?' she inquired.

'I have been away for such a long time, I have lost all association to the cedi. How much do you think we should give him?'

'One Ghana cedi, an equivalent of 10000 old cedis.'

'Okay, go ahead. I will refund it later.'

She pulled her purse from her handbag, unzipped it and handed him a bright red newly printed bank note.

'Take that; one Ghana cedi!' she said and handed it to him.

'Thank you sir, Massa! I would have preferred dollars though!'

'When did we start using the dollar as currency in this country?' I inquired.

'Massa, some dollars, please!' he persisted.

'You be satisfied with what you have got!' Joyce told him. 'Please follow me: we have parked the Taxi several metres away from here,' she said after the stranger had left us alone.

At that moment, a young man aged about thirty approached us.

'Come and join my car: I have parked it at the other end of the road. Wait as I hurry to fetch it.' So saying, he walked briskly away.

'Be careful, uncle!' Joyce began in reaction to the offer from the stranger.

'These days there are a lot of tricksters and thieves roaming the city.'

'We still need a second vehicle; one taxi will not be enough to carry the six of us plus our luggage.'

Soon we were all gathered around the cab Joyce had hired, an ageing Toyota saloon car. Moments later the strange young man pulled his vehicle alongside us. I noticed that his vehicle, a Toyota Corolla estate car, was painted uniformly red, not the traditional yellow plus a second colour associated with local taxis. Soon we began to pack our items into both cars.

We were then faced with the issue of where to go. Since there had been no sign of anyone from the hotel at the airport, we thought Kwasi had probably not accessed his e-mails the previous evening and was thus in the dark regarding the change in our flight schedule.

That we could not follow Joyce to Tema to rest at the place where she lived was clear to me. A second year student of the University of Cape Coast, she was spending her holidays at Tema. She was staying together with several other members of the extended family in a garage assigned to Ransford's flat. At the time when the refurbishing began on the main flat, the garage was converted into makeshift accommodation to house the few residents of the main flat until such time as a permanent solution could be found. Despite its limited space, it had in the meantime attracted several other members of the family who had moved from the countryside into the city in search of work.

In the end we decided to head for the Teshie-Nungua Estate at Nungua, a suburb to the south east of the city. Prior to her departure for Europe, Rita lived with her uncle and his German wife in one of the houses on the estate. It was a large detached home boasting a large surrounding compound. Following her uncle's death several years ago and the subsequent return of his ex-wife to Germany, the building became occupied by several members of the extended family who had moved from her hometown to the national capital for various reasons. That would be a convenient place of rest until we were able to make contact with the hotel.

'Okay, boys and girls, let's get going,' I began. 'We must form two groups. The first group, including Rita, will drive ahead. The rest will follow in the second vehicle.' The children joined their mother in the first vehicle whilst Joyce and I drove in the second. Moments later the taxi driver set his vehicle in motion. Just then the driver of the second vehicle, whom we had taken for any other driver shuttling passengers to and from the airport, turned to me and asked,

'Why the need, sir, to drive first to Teshie-Nungua?'

'We want to rest there until we can get in touch with the hotel where we are to stay.'

'But I have been sent by the hotel to pick you up!'

'That just cannot be true!' I cried on top of my voice.

'Yes, indeed! I am the driver of the hotel. We got the message that you were due to arrive in the morning, so I was sent to pick you up.'

'Why then didn't you make it clear from the beginning?'

'I held the board bearing your name at the entrance. I thought you understood it!'

Yes indeed, despite the hectic excitement and confusion surrounding our arrival, I had spotted a young man in the crowd holding a board on which my name was boldly written. Thinking he was the driver of the vehicle Joyce had brought to pick us up, I did not make much of it.

29

'No, I took you for the driver of the cab I had asked my niece to meet me with! As it is, I saw her several years ago when she was only a young girl. I thought *they* brought the board along to help connect with each other!' I had to rethink our plans! 'Be quick! Let us chase them and give them a sign to follow us instead of the other way round.'

As we drove away from the airport, one thing caught my attention, namely the absence of a large statue of General Kotoka, one of the architects of the 1966 coup which overthrew the first post-independent civilian government headed by President Nkrumah. He was killed in a failed counter-coup in 1967. Not long afterwards, his statue was erected about a hundred metres in front of the main airport building. The international airport was also named after him.

'Where is the statue?' I asked the driver, who had in the meantime introduced himself as Tetteh.

'It was removed a few years ago to make room for the expansion and refurbishment of the airport,' he replied.

Shortly afterwards we caught up with the others. Our driver blew his horn, signalled with his headlamps and also gesticulated for them to stop. The other driver soon got the message and pulled to a stop by the roadside. We drove past them, signalling them to follow us; the confusion in their faces was clearly visible.

We turned right at the Airport Junction and drove along the broad three-lane dual carriageway leading towards Legon, a northern suburb of the city. I was impressed by the state of the road. Thirteen years ago, it was a one-track road used by traffic flowing in both directions.

After following the road for about a kilometre we turned right just after emerging from under the Tetteh Quarshie Overpass. The overpass was also new to me: thirteen years ago, the spot where it had been constructed was a roundabout bearing the same name and noted for considerable congestion.

The branch road we followed led to a roundabout that we left at the second exit to join a very busy road—the Spintex Road. As we drove along this road the unfamiliar scene unfolding before my eyes made me feel like someone who had just arrived in a strange city.

On huge billboards placed on each side of the road, trade names entirely new to me—GT-Mobile, Fidelity Bank, Stanbic Bank, Cal Bank, etc.—were advertising their products and services.

I was particularly struck by several billboards along the way displaying the advertisement of financial institutions urging customers to apply for a loan—'Apply today, Get your decision tomorrow!' Thirteen years ago it was unthinkable to read such open invitations to apply for a loan from any bank in the country.

The road was lined on each side with newly constructed buildings housing small and large retail shops dealing in all kinds of wares ranging from washing machines, gas/electric cookers, refrigerators, deep freezers, rice, flour, etc., small wholesale, retail and grocery shops as well as large wholesale shops dealing in all kinds of goods.

As we drove further and further along the road, through an area completely unknown to me, I could no longer keep my curiosity to myself.

'Where are we now?' I asked the driver.

'This area is a relatively new settlement generally referred to as the Spintex Road, though, strictly speaking, it is only the road we are driving on that is known by that name. Settlements stretch for a distance of about twelve kilometres on either side of the road.'

After driving on the road over a distance of about ten kilometres, the driver turned left into a less busy road. We followed this branch road for about half a kilometre until it ended at a T-junction. From there the driver turned right onto a rough road, the condition of which contrasted starkly from those we had so far been following.

Not only was the road untarred, it was very uneven and on the surface displayed several large potholes. As a result of the downpour in the morning, the holes had become ponds of water. Jonathan subsequently christened this stretch of road *The Muddy Street*. Painstakingly the driver swerved frequently to avoid one pool of water after another.

The state of the road contrasted greatly with the buildings found on each side of it, the majority of which were mansions of the executive class.

In the course of my stay, I noticed that the situation I had just described was not isolated but characteristic of a phenomenon that could be observed in several of the newly developed areas of the city. Apparently the rate at which new residential estates are springing up outpaces the ability to provide the amenities to service such areas. Hence it is not uncommon to find areas that boast newly constructed posh mansions linked by makeshift roads of the type mentioned. Amenities such as tap water, electricity and telephone are also not always available in such areas. The builders seem prepared to put up their houses in un-serviced areas in anticipation of future service provisions.

After travelling about half a kilometre on *Muddy Street* the driver finally pulled up in front of the gate of a magnificent modern two-storey building brightly painted in rose-pink. Somehow someone in the building saw the hotel car approaching for no sooner had we pulled up there than someone swung the gate open. The driver parked the car on the large paved compound within the concrete walls.

We were warmly greeted by the staff who briskly helped transport our luggage to our rooms on the first floor. Originally we were promised the semi-detached building with the self-catering facilities. We were told on arrival, however, that owing to an oversight on the part of the staff, the property had been double- booked. The only consolation was that we were promised the facility on our return to Accra to prepare for our return to the UK after our tour of the countryside. Lena's Inn, as the hotel is known, boasts of ten rooms. We were assigned to Rooms 101 and 110, by virtue probably of the fact that they were almost opposite to each other. Each of the spacious rooms was fully furnished and boasts floors decorated with beautiful high quality ceramic and terrazzo. The bath and toilet facilities in each room were of excellent quality.

Each room had the benefit of satellite TV as well as wireless Internet access. The latter proved particularly useful to me, enabling me not only to keep abreast with the outside world but also to book working sessions with my agencies in the UK. I thought to myself that if the quality of the Internet facility in the hotel was a yardstick to go by, then Ghana might be considered to have positioned itself very favourably as far as the global village of the World Wide Web was concerned.

CHAPTER 5
Pizza for Three

﷽

Having solved the problem of accommodation, the next important issue to tackle was that of transportation. During my previous visits, I had either used the vehicle of my brother Ransford or one that I had shipped several weeks prior to my departure from Europe. Ransford cleared them and got them registered before my arrival. Since he was no longer living in the country, this time I decided against sending any vehicle. I wanted to spare myself the headache of having to clear the vehicle from the harbour personally. The process is so cumbersome and time consuming that one is better advised to leave it in the hands of someone conversant with the system. Even with all his 'expertise' Ransford on one occasion was unable to clear a used vehicle at the harbour for me. The import duty was so high that it was almost equal to double the money I spent on purchasing it! In the end I decided to leave it to the state; only God knows what happened to it.

Kwasi initially arranged the hire of a Toyota 4x4 at a comparatively favourable rate. Shortly before our arrival, however, things ran into difficulty. The owner of the vehicle, a dealer in second-hand vehicles, had left the country on a business tour of Asia. His wife, unaware of the arrangement between her husband and Kwasi, was unwilling to release it to him. He passed the message on to his brother-in-law and owner of our accommodation, and pleaded with him to help us find another vehicle. He promised to do what he could to help. In the interim, he instructed Tetteh to drive us around with the hotel vehicle until such time that we could find our own means of transport.

In the meantime we were busy at work unpacking our items and getting used to our two rooms. Suddenly Jonathan ran to his mother.

'Mama,' he cried, 'I am hungry.'

'Really?'

'Yes indeed.'

How could we satisfy the immediate desire of the youngest member of the group? I was certain we could find a chop bar nearby (fast food restaurant) offering local dishes such a *yokogarri, waakye, omo tuo, banku, fufu*. That would not be something he would be looking for, however—not on his first day in the country. There was another issue that needed to be tackled—we needed to exchange some of the 'queens heads'—as Charles, my Nigerian friend, a GP working in the UK, calls the pound—into local currency.

Just as we were considering what to do, I took a look through the window. My eyes caught sight of the driver who was busy hand-washing the car. I wondered why he was taking the trouble to do that, considering that he would be driving on *Muddy Street* several times that day. I decided to go downstairs and ask him if he could take us to a bank where we could exchange our money.

'No problem!' he began on hearing what I had to say. 'Just let me know when you are ready. The manager has instructed me to take you to wherever you wish. I only need to let Madam, his wife, know about my whereabouts.'

'That is very nice of him,' I replied.

'When do you want to leave?'

'Whenever you are ready. Jonathan, my little boy, is hungry.'

'Okay, you get ready. In the meantime I will go and inform Madam who lives in the house just on the other side of the road that I am taking you to town.' He pointed to an elegant executive mansion on the other side of the road about a hundred metres from the hotel.

Just then it occurred to me that there would be seven passengers travelling— the five of us, Joyce and himself!

'Could you please find a second vehicle? I will pay for it.'

'What for, sir?' he inquired, somewhat surprised.

'There won't be enough space in this one for seven of us.'

'No bother, sir; we'll manage—the little boy and you will sit beside me in the front; Madam and the rest will be at the back.'

Soon all of us were crammed into the hotel car. Jonathan had in the end to sit on my lap. I looked at his face for his reaction and realised he was not amused by the arrangement! Back in the UK he would have insisted he sat on his own child safety seat. If only for the first few days of our stay he had no choice but to 'do in Rome what the Romans do.'

We drove back along *Muddy Street* back unto the Spintex Road. Our first place of call was a forex bureau. For the sake of convenience the country had just re-denominated the national currency, the cedi. In the process, four zeros had been shed. That meant that 10000 old cedis were now equivalent to 1 Ghana cedi, as the new currency was known.

We exchanged two hundred pounds to start with. That came up to approximately 3.6 million cedis, or 360 Ghana cedis. I requested the old notes rather than the new ones. The motive behind my request was simple economics—since I expected relatives, friends and even strangers to be asking me for money wherever I went, the old and less valuable notes would help me fulfil their desires without us feeling the pinch too much. On the other hand, handing someone even a one Ghana cedi note would imply giving that person 10000 old cedis, something I would probably not have done.

'I am afraid I have to disappoint you, sir,' the cashier began. 'The banks have ceased supplying us with old cedi notes.'

Well, there was no way out! It was up to me to know how best to deal with those who appealed to me for assistance.

The twenty-Ghana-cedi note bore such a close resemblance to the newly introduced twenty-pound note in the UK that I began to wonder whether it had been printed by the same firm!

Seeing I had been handed only a few Ghana cedi notes for the equivalent of 3.6 million cedis, Tetteh remarked:

'That is brilliant, doc!'

'Why?'

'Do you know what? Before the re-denomination, you would have needed a large plastic bag to carry home your money. Now 3.6 million cedis can fit into a normal wallet. I must confess, though, that I am yet to begin thinking in terms of the new currency. I am so used to dealing in the old that it will take me some time to adjust.'

'Well, you have six months to do so,' the cashier came in. 'After that you will have no choice, for by then only the new notes will be in circulation.'

Having equipped ourselves with the local medium of exchange, we turned our attention to the children.

'Could you please help us out to find something for the children to eat, Tetteh?' I began.

'Do your children like pizza?' he inquired

'Oh, yes, we really enjoy pizza!' Karen came in.

'That is great. There is a modern fast food restaurant around the corner; they offer pizzas.'

'A pizza hut in today's Ghana!' I exclaimed.

'Doc, now one can buy almost anything in the country. One only has to have the means to do so!'

He took us to a newly built Total Filling station. Several metres from it, on the same premises, was a building which accommodated several fast food restaurants as well as a grocery shop.

One thing struck me when I read the prices of the meals, drinks and other items on sale there—they were being sold at prices that were almost identical with those offered in the UK. A large pizza, for example, was being sold for 45000 cedis, that is almost five US dollars.

This should be seen in the light of the fact that the minimum wage of the country is around two dollars a day. If only this kind of pricing could be restricted to items such as pizzas, which might be regarded as luxury items by the common man on the street! Unfortunately this is not the case; foodstuffs for local consumption, while abundant, are sold at relatively high prices.

As we got out of the vehicle, my attention was drawn to an ATM built into a massive concrete structure on one corner of the premises of the filling station. ATM machines in Ghana! I wondered whether it was for only local usage or whether it accepted international cards such as Visa and America Express. I decided to find out for myself by trying to withdraw money with a Visa debit card issued by my UK bank.

I inserted it and waited anxiously for the response. I was asked to key in my four-digit PIN Number. I complied. Next I pressed the knob pointing to 100 Ghana cedis. A short while later, out popped twenty freshly printed five Ghana cedi notes! It had indeed worked! It was a really marvellous surprise.

However, someone might argue: 'But an ATM machine does not solve the poverty of the common man on the street in Accra!'

Of course it wouldn't. My opinion, though, is that it can contribute, even if in a small way, to make Ghana attractive to international business. Attraction of investment, both foreign and local, could help generate wealth that in turn could create jobs that could help people out of poverty.

Karen & Co were so impressed by the quality of the pizza offered that we made a regular stop there for lunch for the most part of our stay in Accra. In time our faces became so well known to the attendants that they became aware of even a day's absence on our part!

CHAPTER 6
Short-lived Joy

Early the next morning we were getting ready to go down for breakfast when the phone in our room began to ring. I was greeted by the voice of one of the staff of the hotel.

'Manager is waiting for you downstairs,' she began. 'He wants to have a word with you.'

'I will be there in a minute,' I replied. Soon I was hurrying downstairs.

I was greeted by Kwasi's brother-in-law who introduced himself by his first name Ridley. Later I got to know that he is also affectionately known as Junior. I put his age at around 35 years. He was simple-looking and modestly dressed. He was not alone; beside him was a gentleman of about his age.

'Doc, I have brought someone who I believe will be able to help you solve your transportation problem,' he announced. 'I will leave you two to sort things out. I have to leave for work.'

'I thought this is your only engagement?' I remarked on hearing him.

'No, I work full time at a Government Department.'

'You must be a very busy man.'

'Well, I do my best,' he said and made for the door.

I turned to the stranger. 'As you might have been told by Manager, I am on a five-week holiday with my family. We intend to travel around the country to visit our respective families. We are looking for a reliable vehicle to rent—one with space for the five of us as well as our luggage. We would prefer a mini-bus.'

'I am able to offer you a Daewoo mini-bus,' he replied without hesitation.

'Brilliant! What is the daily rate?'

'100 dollars. For security reasons we normally insist our vehicles are driven by our own drivers. They cost an additional 10 dollars per day, but since you have been introduced by my friend, I am prepared to entrust it to you directly. That will save you the driver's fee.'

'100 dollars is a considerable sum. I am prepared to pay 60.'

'That is unacceptable. You are welcome to shop around to find out for yourself what other firms are demanding.'

'Still, 100 dollars is too high a price. Consider the fact that we shall be keeping it for about thirty days.'

'Well, you may have it for 80 dollars.'

'This is modern day Ghana! You no longer deal in cedis?'

'When did you last visit here?'

'I am ashamed to reveal it—I have not been here since October 1994!'

'That is indeed a long time. Ghana has changed considerably; yes, indeed, many firms now demand dollars in their transactions.'

I paused for a while to consider the offer. A minibus to transport us comfortably around the country at a cost of $80 US dollars a day, the equivalent of £45 at the then current exchange rate—it might be considered a good deal, I reasoned. For the comfort of the children in particular, I decided to go for it. (I pictured how David would fare in a typically crowded *tro-tro!*[1])

'Please give me some time to organise it,' he replied after I had made my intention known to him. 'You will hear from me in due course.'

Just as we were about to part he turned to me again.

'Do you have a Ghana mobile number?'

'Yes. We bought a SIM card yesterday.'

'Please let me have it.'

After he had stored it on his phone, we parted company. The whole family was delighted at the prospect of having a vehicle at our disposal;

---

[1] *Tro-tro is the main form of transport within cities and towns of the country. They usually consist of mini-buses operated by private hands.*

it meant there was no longer any need to bother Tetteh with pleas to drive us around.

Our joy was short-lived, for barely an hour after his departure the stranger called to inform us the bus was no longer available. As an alternative he offered us a pick-up with seats for five persons and an open compartment for goods at the same daily rate. I promptly rejected the offer. The disappointment on our faces at the sudden twist of events was clearly evident.

What was to be done?

I decided to seek the advice of Tetteh who was relaxing in the hotel vehicle parked at the usual place in front of the hotel.

'There are several car rental firms around,' he said on hearing the news. 'We can drive around and look for a suitable one to rent.'

'Are you still allowed to drive us around?'

'Yes, indeed. Manager told me as he was leaving for work to do just that, provided it suits the plans of Madam. So please wait while I go to check.'

He returned after about five minutes from the gated property, smiling.

'I have been given the green light. We have to be back by 15:00 hrs though. I need to pick up the kids from school.'

We needed to hurry. It was already a few minutes past ten. I hurried upstairs to get everyone ready.

'I suggest we first try Tema,' said Joyce, who had in the meantime joined us. 'I have come across a few car rental firms there.'

The driver agreed, if only on practical grounds. 'That way we shall avoid the congestion that has likely built up on the Spintex Road at this time of day,' he stated.

After barely ten minutes' drive our attention was drawn to a mini-bus parked by the roadside with a large board that carried the bold FOR RENTAL sign placed on top of it.

'Please pull up by the roadside and let me have a look,' I said to the driver. Jonathan and the driver accompanied me while the rest remained behind. A middle-aged man, about forty-five, emerged from a shop near where the vehicle was parked.

'We have just arrived from the UK,' I told him. 'We are looking for a vehicle of this type to take us around.'

'Where in the UK?'

'Loughborough.'

'Where is that?'

'A few kilometres to the north of Leicester.'

'I used to live in London. Indeed, my wife and the children are still there. We all came over to settle here. She and the children decided to return after a while. I would have liked the children to remain here, to learn discipline and wisdom. London is not the best of place to bring up a child.'

Without responding directly to that, I went straight to business.

'What is your daily rate?'

'120 dollars plus an additional 20 dollars a day for the driver!'

'But I can drive it myself.'

'No way, friend! For security reasons we insist on our own driver for our vehicles!'

'No coming down on the price?'

'No, sir.'

He must be a hard-bargainer, I thought. There was no way I would agree to that price. Still, I decided to be diplomatic.

'Well, we will consider the offer and come back to you should the need arise.'

Soon we were back on the road to Tema. In the end our effort proved futile. Joyce was indeed right in her information. What we found at the place she had in mind, however, was only a signpost bearing the bold letters CAR RENTAL. An arrow indeed did point in a certain direction. Those we spoke to in the area could only recall a firm that had stopped operating several months ago. Someone who got to know what had brought us there re-directed us to Labadi, a suburb of Accra.

'There, along the Ring Road, you will find several rental firms to choose from,' he added.

The time in the meantime was 11:30 hrs. Just then an idea flashed through my mind, namely, to purchase a used mini-bus instead of renting one! It was not a bad idea, I reasoned. At the end of our stay we could either resell it or find a reliable person to place in his/her custody to be used as a *tro-tro*. Proceeds could be used to support my ageing father as well as our respective extended family members. I made my intention known to the rest of the group.

'That is a superb idea, Doc!' Tetteh remarked on hearing that. 'You are unlikely to get a suitable vehicle to rent for a daily rate below 100 dollars. Add to that an additional 10 dollars minimum daily rate for the driver. That would add up to 3300 dollars for the thirty days you want it for. That in my opinion is money thrown to the wind!'

'What do you think, Joyce?' I inquired from my shy-looking niece.

'She cannot be objective in her judgement!' Rita came to her rescue. 'As a member of the extended family, she will after all be a beneficiary of your plan,' she added.

'Still, I find it a wonderful idea,' Joyce joined in.

'I will go for a purchase, Tetteh, if only you could take us to a place where we could select from many.'

'I will drive you to an area not far from the Kwame Nkrumah Circle. There are several second-hand car dealers there. Maybe you can find what you are looking for.'

Soon we were heading back towards Accra.

CHAPTER 7
Two Famous Sons of Ghana

A s we left the Spintex Road and joined the main highway heading towards Accra my attention was drawn to a newly constructed magnificent five-storey building on the right-hand side of the road, not far from the junction with the peculiar name, HIPC Junction. (How the junction came to be associated with this abbreviation—standing for 'Heavily Indebted Poor Countries'—is a mystery to me!)

'Ghanaians are putting up posh buildings these days!' I remarked, pointing to the building complex.

'That building, Doc, is not devoid of controversy!' Tetteh stressed.

'Which controversy?'

'Well, many in the country associate it with our current president, President John Kufuor.'

'Why?'

'They allege it belongs to him.'

Just then I recalled reading on the Internet several months ago about a building the Ghanaian opposition alleged belonged to the president, something he vehemently denied. He asserted instead that it belonged to his elder son.

'Is it the so-called Kufour Hotel?' I inquired.

'Yes indeed!'

'I read about it on the Internet about two years ago. What evidence do those linking it with the president have to prove their case?'

'Well, it is the usual *yesee, yesee* (Twi for rumours, hearsay, gossip and allegations).

'Ghanaians and *yesee*, *yesee*!' I shook my head, smiling, recalling in particular the period between the middle and late seventies. At that time Ghana was under the rule of General Acheampong. Rumour regarding corruption, nepotism, embezzlement of funds in high places as well as persecution of the opposition was so widespread in the country that one could hardly separate rumour from fact.

'Well, as far as that habit is concerned, things have not changed much over the years, doc! It was so during Acheampong's regime. It was so during the time of Rawlings, and so it is today! One does not easily have to dismiss such rumours though; as the saying goes, behind every rumour is an element of truth.'

'Has the hotel gone into operation?' I wanted to know

'Yes; it did so about two years ago. It operates under the official name African Regency Hotel, although almost everyone here calls it Kufuor Hotel. Indeed, many a citizen here does not take the president by his word when he denies ownership. In their eyes he is using his son as a cover-up.'

The driver made a detour at the Airport junction. Instead of driving straight on, he turned left and headed for the Airport.

'What are you up to?' I inquired.

'I want to buy fuel at my favourite filling station around the corner.'

As he drove away from the filling station after filling his tank, Tetteh pointed to another attractive multi-storey building with prominent large blue glass windows. The building bore the inscription UNA House.

'That building belongs to Kofi Annan,' he remarked

'I know the term UNA stands for United Nations Association, so no doubt it's possible he will pop up there from time to time—but are you sure that it is his *own* property?'

'Well Doc, the usual *yesee*, *yesee*,' he replied laughing.

I took the opportunity to inquire from Tetteh about the latest in regard to the former UN Secretary General, the famous son of the country. A few months prior to our arrival I had read an account on the Internet concerning his triumphal homecoming. People from all walks of life thronged the airport to bid the national hero *akwaaba (*welcome).

'Do you hear or read about him these days?' I wanted to know.

'Only during the first few weeks of his return. Since then he has maintained a relatively low profile.'

'The other day I read about an opinion poll which seems to suggest he could win the presidential race should he decide to contest it.'

'Well, since his arrival he has on several occasions had to answer questions relating to his presidential ambitions. As far as I know he has on all such occasions categorically ruled out that prospect.'

'Should he decide to run he will have my vote. He could use his extensive international connections for the good of the country.'

'On the other hand, becoming involved in the *tschooboye, tschooboye* (hurly-burly) of Ghanaian politics is not without risks. It could eventually tarnish his image and soil his good reputation

CHAPTER 8
Display of Majesty

꙰

As we headed towards the Kwame Nkrumah Circle my attention was drawn to a huge billboard mounted not far away from perhaps the most well-known intersection in the whole country. After the coup that overthrew the Nkrumah regime in 1966 everything associated with him and his party, the CPP, was banned. The Kwame Nkrumah Circle was renamed National Liberation Circle or Liberation Circle for short. As a result of the increasing recognition of the role of the man who led Ghana to independence and chartered the course of the African, however, the circle has been allowed to revert to its original name.

The giant billboard displayed an equally huge picture depicting President Kufuor of Ghana and Queen Elisabeth II of England. I immediately recognised the picture as one of those taken a few months earlier during the Ghanaian President's state visit to the UK and published in several UK newspapers.

The circumstances that led to the state visit had earlier on generated political debate in the country.

To mark the 50th anniversary of the country's independence from British rule on 6th March 1957, the government had declared the whole year the year of national celebration. The climax was to be on 6th March when a huge parade was to be held at Independence Square.

Several World leaders and dignitaries were invited. The government extended an invitation to the Queen. Buckingham Palace turned it down and decided instead to send Prince Andrew to represent his mother.

Instead, in what was described as a recognition of the important relationship between the two countries, the Queen invited the Ghanaian president to a three-day state visit shortly after the celebrations in Accra.

The matter was interpreted differently by the government and the opposition. While the former read in the gesture a recognition of the increasing importance of the country on the international scene, the latter regarded it as an affront. To them the Head of the Commonwealth should have attended in person such an august event that marked the 50th Anniversary of the first African country to gain independence from her country.

President Kufour's state visit got underway on the 13th of March with a spectacular ceremony in Buckingham palace. The climax came when the Ghanaian leader and the British Monarch climbed into the Centuries-old, Gold State Coach pulled by eight horses and led by 100 others, for the carriage procession to the Grand Entrance of the Palace.

The portrait of the two prominent personalities boldly on display on the streets of Accra bore an equally bold heading:

MAJESTIC

There is currently in Ghana a vibrant political culture. The two main parties, the ruling New Patriotic Party (NPP) and the opposition National Democratic Congress (NDC) seem constantly to be on the lookout for opportunities to either score political points or display the other in a poor light before the electorate. I decided long before my visit to the country to keep myself above politics. Still, I could not restrain my mind from pondering on the huge billboard that confronted my eyes.

What would the proverbial common man on the street, who, judging from what I had observed during our stay was struggling to make ends meet despite the remarkable improvement I have already referred to, make of the spending of public money in that manner?

Would he/she share my view that the money so spent could better have been invested in projects that could be beneficial to his/her cause? Or would he/she reason differently and take the view that considering the immensity of the problem he/she is exposed to daily, the money so spent would in effect have amounted to a mere drop in a huge, huge ocean?

CHAPTER 9
The Missing Shock Absorber

F inally we came to the area the driver had in mind. Even as we approached the place in the car, my attention was drawn to a mini Mercedes bus, painted brightly dark-orange, parked on the premises of one of the dealers.

'That seems quite attractive,' I told Tetteh. 'Let's give it a closer look.' Just as we drew near to the mini-bus several young men, average age about 35 years, approached us from all directions.

'Massa, what kind of vehicle are you looking for?' they inquired as if with a single voice.

Even before I could answer one of them drew closer to me, a smile on his face.

'Do you recognise me, Massa?'

'No; who are you?'

'You are from Amantia, right or wrong?'

'Yes indeed, that is my mother's hometown.'

'I know you very well! I used to be a friend of your brother Thomas. He is currently resident in Holland, right or wrong?'

'Right!' I replied

'What are you doing here?'

I let him know what had brought us there.

'That indeed is a very good vehicle,' he said, indicating the mini-bus. 'I will recommend it.'

Just then he began to look around. 'Hey, CK, where are you?' he called out. 'I have found a customer for you. Give him a good deal—he is from my home village!' (As I learnt later on, these young men, mostly unemployed, hang around the car dealers looking around for potential buyers. They receive a token commission from the owner should their mediation lead to a purchase.)

Soon the owner, whose age I put at about forty-five, emerged from behind one of several vehicles parked in the yard.

'How much is this bus selling for?'

'140 million cedis,' he replied. 'Oh, I forgot that we now have to think in the re-denominated currency. Well, 14000 Ghana cedis, or approximately 14000 US dollars.'

'How old is it?'

'Not very old, sir; it is in top condition. Originally it was a delivery van lacking any seats. We have fitted the seats after clearing them from the harbour. Excellent job, isn't it? You buy it today and it is ready for the road tomorrow. I advise you to look out for a good driver. In 12 months at the latest you will have recovered the money you spent to purchase it!'

'It is not intended for use as *tro tro*,' I told him. 'At least, not in the immediate future.'

'What do you need it for?'

'For use by the family during our stay in the country.'

'Where do you live?'

'In the UK. We are here on holiday.'

'That will be a very comfortable vehicle for the family. The children could sleep comfortably in it should they feel like doing so while you are on your way. So Massa, help us by purchasing it—the Market is not very good. I have not been able to sell anything for several days!'

At that stage our driver set out to examine it—first the engine, then the inside as well and the underside, lying almost flat on the ground to get a good view.

'It is in quite a good condition,' he began after a thorough inspection. 'I have noticed a weak point, however.'

'What have you noticed?' CK came in, somehow irritated.

'The shock absorber of one of the rear wheels has been removed!'

'Hey, friend, are you an auto mechanic?' CK burst out, clearly caught on the wrong foot.

'That is the reason I brought him!' I stated

'I had not noticed it,' CK said after inspecting it himself. 'It could have been removed at the harbour. That should not be a problem though. We need first to agree on the price. I will replace it at my own expense.'

'Doc, before you bargain on a price, let them take us on a test drive,' Tetteh suggested

'You go with them, I will wait for you. I will buy it only on your recommendation.'

Moments later one of CK's assistants, who only introduced himself as Mohammed, was speeding away in the mini-bus, Tetteh in the passengers seat beside him.

They returned after about twenty minutes.

'Doc, it is in good condition,' Tetteh affirmed. 'I will recommend it.'

Just then an idea occurred to me to inspect the reading on the speedometer. It stood at 145000 KM.

On seeing me CK began, 'You burgers[21] are not easy to deal with! Over here hardly anyone takes the speedometer reading into consideration when purchasing a vehicle.'

In the end we settled on a price of 135 Million cedis (13500 Ghana cedis or approximately 13500 dollars). That included the money to be spent on the registration. Then arose the issue of how I was going to come by the amount needed for the purchase. I had made room in our calculation for a rental vehicle at a daily rate of about 80 dollars; now I had to top up that by a sum of about 10000 dollars.

I still had some funds in my account in the UK to meet the cost. In the short run, however, I would have to use all the money we had in Ghana. Thanks to the Internet, I could transfer funds into the account of a close associate in the UK and ask him to use the services of a global fast money transfer service to get money across to us as soon as possible.

In the end it was agreed that I pay half the amount the next day, and the rest by the end of the following week.

---

2   Burger, short for Hamburger—a term generally used to refer to a Ghanaian back home after a stay in the West.

For the vehicle to be reserved overnight, CK demanded a token payment. Since we had not reckoned with the transaction, we had left much of the money we exchanged the previous day at the hotel. Eventually he agreed to keep the £120 left in my wallet for the night.

The next day we ran into difficulty fulfilling our part of the deal. We had converted our money into travellers' cheques and had purchased about ninety percent of them from the travel agent, Thomas Cook. Whilst on a visit to South Africa two years earlier, we were able to change them without difficulty. Whereas everyone was prepared to exchange the cheques that bore only the trademark *American Express*, no other financial institution was prepared to exchange those that bore the additional name *Thomas Cook,* something that surprised a layman like me. The only explanation the banks gave was that they had an unresolved issue with the travel company.

Yet another hindrance: I was told by the banks that the maximum amount of travellers' cheques one could exchange per day was 250 dollars. Eventually we were helped by the Standard Chartered Bank which carried out what they referred to as 'swapping'. By this means one could withdraw a maximum of three thousand dollars from each of the bank's branches per day on a debit or credit card.

Although I could not hand out fifty percent of the purchase price when we turned up the next day, Friday, CK agreed to hand the keys over to me. Besides that, he gave me a red registration number, which, according to him, I could use for seven days. At long last, after two days of 'parasiting' on the hotel car, we had our own means of transport!

I was advised by some not to drive on my own, but rather to entrust the driving to someone else. Driving on the roads in Accra in particular and the country in general could be very challenging, particularly for one used to driving in Western Europe. Counting on my experience from previous visits, however, I decided to do it myself.

Soon we were stuck in the busy traffic in and around the Kwame Nkrumah Circle. I switched over from the practice of driving in Europe where one insists on one's rights whilst on the road, and reverted to what I term 'consensus driving'. Soon I came to a traffic light; it was not functional due to a power outage in the area. The traffic wardens were yet to arrive on the scene.

'*P-e-p-e-e-p-e! P-e-p-e-e-p-e!! P-e-p-e-e-p-e!!!*
'*P-a-p-a-a-p-a! P-a-p-a-a-p-a!! P-a-p-a-a-p-a!!!*
'*P-u-p-u-u-p-u! P-u-p-u-u-p-u!! P-u-p-u-u-p-u!!!*' came the sound of horns from all directions as one driver after the other tried to draw the attention of the other to their intention to cross.

I tried to do the same. My horn would not sound! We had overlooked that when we were testing it. (I learnt later, when I pulled up at a fitting shop to have the problem sorted out, that the main component had been removed!) Devoid of a horn, I had to resort to my voice as and when necessary to plead with other drivers to give me way! My head stretched out of the open window, I would resort to shouting at the top of my voice in *Twi*: '*Awuraa* (Madam), *Owura* (Mister), *Menuabaa* (Sister), *Menuabarima* (Brother), *meserewo, ma me kwan!* (Please give way)!'

After shedding a considerable amount of sweat, I finally put the approximately twenty-kilometre distance between the Nkrumah Circle and Lena's Inn behind me.

CHAPTER 10
Supermarket Accra

A s we drove through the city of Accra, it appeared to me as if much of it had become a sort of pedestrian market with goods of all sorts and makes on sale. That is not to say that the streets of the city had ever been free from petty traders and street hawkers. Indeed, street trading has always been a hallmark of life in Accra . What struck me on this visit was the extraordinary dimensions this form of trade had assumed. Traders offering goods for sale could be seen virtually everywhere on the street.

There were several aspects of the trade. There were the typical street hawkers roaming up and down the streets carrying their wares on their heads, shoulders, arms, hands, backs and what-have-you with the hope of finding buyers for their wares. There were also those who displayed their wares on tables, wooden structures, kiosks as well as other makeshift stands placed on the edges of the roads and streets.

Although the street hawkers could be found almost everywhere, they were particularly conspicuous in and around areas prone to traffic congestion such as both sides of the stretch of road bordering busy intersections as well as in and around major transport depots.

During the morning and evening rush hours, when the roads tend to be particularly congested, the streets are rarely clear of them as they move between slowly moving traffic looking for opportunities to sell their goods direct to the drivers or their passengers.

Where traffic is quick moving, they hang around the roadside waiting for the lights to turn red or the police officers directing traffic to signal oncoming traffic to halt. Then they see their chance and pour onto the streets to present their wares to the travellers.

Not only adults, including in some cases mothers carrying their babies at their backs, are engaged in the trade; boys and girls, some barely ten years old as well as teens and young adults of both sexes, are agile participants in the booming merchandising on the streets of Accra.

What wares were on sale? Anything imaginable! In the category foodstuffs one could be offered items such as boiled eggs, freshly baked bread, fried yams, roasted groundnut, bananas, oranges, apples, etc.

The street hawkers seem to have the welfare of travellers as well as pedestrians sweating under the scorching African heat at heart; they offer ice water contained in small plastic bags as well as chilled soft drinks such as Coca Cola, Fanta, Pepsi Cola, Sprite, etc. Those who so wish can also enjoy ice cream from one of several vendors on bikes.

Those who cannot make it to the shopping malls can obtain their toilet rolls, soaps of all kinds and makes, shampoos, toothpaste, toothbrush, cosmetics of all kinds and makes, beverages of all kinds and makes—the list is unending—from the hawkers on the street.

Other items on offer include arts and crafts, T-Shirts, and fan articles! Talking of fan articles! I was particularly struck by a large poster of Drogba, the Ivorian football star of FC Chelsea Football Club, in a pose with an open mouth and outstretched tongue.

'That guy will definitely not be amused to find such an embarrassing pose of himself on sale on the streets of faraway Accra!' I said to myself. Of course, the hawkers had not forgotten the local hero, Michael Essien, also of FC Chelsea fame in their calculation; several posters displaying him in various poses could be obtained.

I could fill pages upon pages with an account of what confronted me in 'Supermarket Accra'. A few spectacular observations and incidents need special mention, however.

As we drove through the streets, not long into our stay, we had to slow down due to traffic congestion. The attention of one of us was drawn to a young man aged about twenty-five standing in the scorching sun by the roadside. Besides him were two dogs, each fastened to a chain he was holding on to. Whereas one of the four-legged creatures could be described as a baby, the other might be classified as a 'teenager' or young 'adult'. The look in their faces betrayed their fear and distress.

'What is he doing with those dogs?' Jonathan inquired.

'Selling them,' Joyce replied.

'But that is not the place to sell dogs!' Karen came in.

'Well, in today's Ghana one can offer anything for sale on the street, provided they are not forbidden,' she remarked, smiling.

'I can imagine a pet lover willing to buy a puppy he or she can train, but not one that has already attained considerable age.'

'Well, he is hopeful of finding someone interested in them, otherwise he wouldn't be here,' Tetteh joined in.

'Let's hope he finds a buyer soon, before they become hungry, lose their temper, and turn their anger on whoever passes by,' Karen added.

On another occasion we were travelling with Nana, Rita's uncle, to an appointment. Nana, who knew the way, drove ahead in his Mercedes saloon car while we followed in our bus.

As we pulled to a stop at a traffic light a young man carrying apples packed in threes in a plastic bag ran up to Nana's vehicle.

'That young man is very conversant with the rules of his trade,' Rita began.

'What do you mean by that?' Karen inquired

'He knows occupants of a Mercedes saloon car are likely to be well-to-do's, who can afford to spend money on imported apples. On the other hand he considers passengers travelling in a bus, which he has taken for a *tro-tro,* are not the kind who would want to spend their money on apples!'

This time round, though, he had miscalculated, for David had in the meantime spotted the delicious looking apples and had stretched his arms towards them! We tried to draw the attention of the seller, but to no avail—he had focussed all his attention on the occupants of the saloon car. They on their part did not seem to be at all interested.

It was only after Nana had pulled away that he became aware of the gesticulations we had all the time been making in his direction. All of a sudden he hurried towards us. Fortunately no vehicles were behind us so we could wait where we were to seal the transaction.

On yet another occasion, as we returned to the hotel after a sight-seeing tour of the city, we decided to purchase some toilet rolls from a hawker who was carrying several bundles, each containing several pieces of the soft tissue. Just before the exchange could be completed, the light turned green. It was a busy street so we couldn't wait. The young man seemed to be familiar with the area.

'Madam, please wait for me at the bus stop ahead of you!' he screamed and gave us the chase of his life!

'We have to honour his efforts,' Rita urged me.

'Yes indeed, it will be cold-hearted on our part not to.'

I turned left at the T-junction a few metres ahead of us into an even busier street. The young man was right; a bus stop was a few metres ahead of us. I pulled to a stop and waited for him. We did not need to wait for long, for no sooner was the vehicle stationary than he caught up with us. The delight in his face was clearly apparent as we exchanged money for his wares.

'That may well be the first sale he has made the whole day!' I remarked.

'And probably his last for the day!' Joyce cut in.

'That cannot go on forever!' I remarked. 'Something has to be done!'

'Everyone needs to survive, Doc!' Joyce stated.

'But that is a waste of potential! So long as this gentleman is young, okay. But he cannot do street hawking all his life. Something indeed needs to be done.'

'Well, that is the situation,' Joyce said in a voice bordering on resignation.

'It should be addressed.'

'By whom?' my niece asked.

'By the government of the day, of course! That is what they were voted to do.'

'In what way?'

'By creating jobs for these young men and women rather than leave them on the street to sell pictures of Drogba, Essien and Co. That is what the Europeans do. They actively create jobs for their unemployed.'

'But they have the means to do so! We are a developing country!'

'I do agree with you, Joyce. In that case we should learn to use our scarce resources effectively. I want to explain my point. As we drove around the city my attention was drawn to the Mercedes limousines of the privileged class. Tetteh told me the limousines were imported just for the 'Ghana @50' celebration, to ferry invited dignitaries around. In my opinion, we could have gone for something cheaper. Well, it isn't too late, is it? Now that the event is over, the government could sell these lavish cars and use the money generated for the benefit of all.'

Just then we drove past several young men and women dressed conspicuously in red working gear, out on the open, trimming the lawns bordering the streets.

'That is an example of job creation, Doc!' Joyce began. 'The government recently recruited several young men and women to plant trees along the streets, to tend the lawns to give the city a facelift and also to contribute to the upkeep of the environment.'

'The intention is laudable. In my opinion, however, our first priority should be to produce abundant and cheap food to feed the population. Indeed, our first priority is surely not to plant trees and lawns that will give Accra a facelift but rather to grow enough food to keep the price of food down.

'I would thus first and foremost channel the energies of the youth engaged in street hawking into agriculture. They could be encouraged to form co-operative agricultural societies. The government should provide them with the start-up capital. Not physical cash, however. No. That form of capital will, with all certainty, drain into porous channels!

'No, the needed capital should be in the form of land, tractors, water spraying machines, animal feed, young birds, sheep, goats, cattle, etc. The beneficiaries could be given a grace period of, say, five years during which time no repayment would be required. Thereafter they could begin repaying in instalments. That would contribute not only to lower the cost of food, but also offer a viable alternative to these young men and women plying their trade on the streets.'

'If only they would be prepared to leave the city for the countryside to do the farming!'

'I believe they will.'

'I am not very sure, uncle!'

'What else do they do when they get to places like Spain?'

'Tell me what they do there, uncle!'

'They are employed on the farms to harvest tomatoes, lettuce, apples, etc.'

'Really?'

'What else did you expect?'

'I thought they would be employed in factories and shops.'

'Not in Spain, young woman. So, if they are prepared to travel all the way to Spain to pick tomatoes, they should be prepared to do so in their own back yard!'

'You should make your ideas known to those in authority.'

'If only they would listen!'

'Well, these days, they seem to care about public opinion.'

CHAPTER 11
Near Suffocation

I was impressed by the significant improvement to the road infrastructure of the city. Several roads that previously were narrow and used by traffic from both directions, had been broadened and converted into dual carriageways boasting two or three lanes in the same direction. Where in former times roundabouts had caused terrible congestions, overpasses have been constructed to facilitate the flow of traffic.

It was in view of the significant overhauling the road network of the city has undergone, that I was struck by the extent of traffic congestion still on the roads. It looked as if the rate at which additional road surfaces were being created was directly proportional to the additional vehicles being registered.

Vehicles of all brands and makes could be found on the roads. The latest brands of the highly valued vehicles, Mercedes, BMW, Jaguar, etc., could be seen driving cheek by jowl with ageing lorries, some of which were in such bad states they might as well be described as death-traps.

A considerable proportion of traffic was made up of *tro-tros* and taxicabs. As we drove around the city, I noticed on several occasions that the *tro-tros* had formed long queues at their collecting points waiting for passengers. That in itself is worthy of mention, representing as it does a significant change compared to former times. Not long ago it was the passengers who queued hours on end in the scorching African heat waiting for the scarce means of transport to bring them to their various destinations.

One particular type of vehicle, the Mercedes D208 minibus, seemed to dominate the *tro-tro* scene. Anyone conversant with the German language could easily make out where the great majority of them had come from, for they still displayed the original German inscriptions of the firms that used to possess them: *Guenthers Malerei Betrieb, Muellers Reinigungsdiesnt, Gas Installation-und Heizungsdiest* etc., they read. It looked as if a considerable proportion of that type of vehicle on display in the yards of second-hand car dealers in Germany eventually end up on the streets of Accra and elsewhere in the country.

'How come almost everyone here seem to prefer the Mercedes D 208 minibus for *tro-tro* use?' I asked Tetteh one day.

'Well, it is said that we Ghanaians are "one-way" people. Someone just need set a trend—and soon you find many of us following suit.

'Several years ago Nissan Urvan mini-buses had a field day here as the preferred vehicle for use as *tro tro*. In the course of time the former was overtaken by the VW LT 35 minibus. Somewhere along the line, someone introduced Mercedes D208 mini-buses into the scene. It proved to be extremely reliable on our rough roads and soon the word began to spread. Before long the pendulum swung in its favour.'

'At any rate, they have contributed towards solving the transportation problem of the city.'

'Indeed they have. Don't give the government credit for the improvement, though. Almost all the used vehicles on the road are brought into the country by individuals—particularly by our citizens resident in Germany, Belgium and Holland. There are other car dealers who travel especially to Europe to buy them on the second-hand market for further shipment into the country.

'Yes, indeed. They have spared the government not only the foreign currency needed to import vehicles to meet our transportation needs, for the state also profits from the taxes levied on them.'

Aggravating the congestion was the countless number of taxicabs on the road. A good proportion were roaming the streets, looking for passengers. That also represented a different picture from what I was used to: several years ago it was passengers who queued in vain for them, not the other way round!

Despite the congestion on the roads, I came across several car dealers in several areas of the city. That also was a new development. During my last visit in 1994 hardly any individual had set up a car-dealing firm. In those days mainly Ghanaians resident in Europe and elsewhere who were visiting brought in the vehicles. They usually registered them for their own personal use during their stay and re-sold them just before they returned to their countries of residence.

The majority of the dealers I came across in today's Ghana dealt in second-hand cars brought in for the most part from Western Europe, a fact that has led some to brand such vehicles 'Eurocarcasses'. Nevertheless, a small proportion of dealers were offering brand new cars for sale.

The congestion on the roads, and seeing vehicles in excellent technical states competing with very worn-out ones, some of which were ripe for the scrapyard, and also seeing the countless number of vehicles on sale on the streets, gave me food for thought. I foresaw a crisis in the making and began to consider ways to avert a possible collapse of traffic, at least in Accra.

As if by coincidence, just as in the case of the street hawkers, a discussion took place just as Joyce was travelling with us. We were travelling to the city when we got stuck in traffic in the scorching sun, behind a worn-out lorry.

'Nothing wrong with standing in the traffic behind a lorry,' someone suggested, no doubt with a touch of cynicism.

'I would agree,' I ventured, 'were it not for the considerable amount of fumes the lorry is pumping almost directly into our vehicle!' Because of the heat and also due to the fact that the vehicle did not possess an air-conditioner, we usually kept several windows open when travelling. Now we were left with the choice to either keep the windows closed and be suffocated in the African heat, or keep some of the windows open and pollute our lungs with the fumes from the truck.

'Why don't they withdraw such death-traps and street polluters from the road!' I cried out in exasperation.

'You want to deprive their owners of their livelihood, uncle!' Joyce countered.

'The safety of the roads should come first, young woman!' I argued. 'This particular vehicle, like several others I have so far observed on the road, is nothing but a time bomb waiting to explode!'

'Well, I doubt the government will be prepared to introduce such an unpopular measure for fear of losing votes!'

'But that is a problem that needs to be solved. They cannot postpone it indefinitely because of the voters.

'Okay,' I conceded, 'I do agree that in the past it was difficult to come across sufficient means of transport. I still recall how often I queued in the scorching sun on the streets of Accra waiting for a *tro tro*. When they finally arrived several were soon filled by queue breakers and those with "connections" to the bookmen (lorry station attendants), leaving us no other choice but to wait and hope for the next vehicle to arrive. When it finally did arrive there was still no guarantee that one would find a seat, even when one stood well ahead of the queue. Now, praise be to God, the reverse is true. There is an abundance of *tro-tros* and taxis are chasing passengers.

'However, this is the time to act! My impression is that in this country, the moment a vehicle is registered, it is allowed to remain in operation until ... only God knows when! Indeed, barring the vehicles being completely damaged through accident or fire, they are allowed to operate until their engines eventually give up the ghost—even in such cases, some owners replace the engines and keep them going.

'It is surprising that such vehicles manage to obtain road worthy certificates! Only recently a leading officer on matters of road safety was bemoaning what he terms the carnage on our roads! What else should one expect when such vehicles are allowed to ply the roads? For the safety of our roads, therefore, all vehicles that do not conform to strict safety requirements should be withdrawn from service.

'There is also another point that needs to be considered, young woman!

'Our country spends a considerable proportion of her foreign earnings on the importation of fuel. By virtue of their age, old vehicles consume more fuel than new ones. The old cars on the road are thus a drain on the national economy.

'And there's yet another issue to consider. We were all forced to breathe the fumes emanating from the truck that was driving ahead of us. We were innocent victims of the prevailing situation. That leads me to the issue of atmospheric pollution in general. These days the talk worldwide is of global warming and what to do to avert further damage to the atmosphere. Reducing the number of such pollutants on our roads will be a contribution in that direction.

'I agree with you on the point you raised, namely what to do with the owners as well as the drivers of the commercial vehicles forced out of service on technical grounds.

'One possible solution is to offer those who fulfil certain criteria new vehicles to replace the old ones on a specially worked out scheme. We will in effect be killing four birds with one stone: we will be contributing to road safety, cutting our fuel bills, reducing atmospheric pollution and preventing others from losing their livelihood.'

'But replacing withdrawn vehicles with new ones will not ease the congestion on the roads that you are bemoaning, uncle!'

'Well, it is likely not everyone will meet the criteria for the replacement of their vehicle; therefore it won't be a one-to-one replacement.

'In the long run, however, we would have to put emphasis on improving the public transportation system—modernise existing rail lines, build new ones, introduce more buses and create bus lanes to facilitate their movement.'

CHAPTER 12
Expansion Without End

I was stunned beyond measure by the extent to which the national capital had grown in size. Without exaggeration, I dare assert that the size of Accra in July 2007 was just about double what it used to be in 1994!

One might say that since the borders of the city had been drawn several years ago, an expansion beyond those borders is not possible. Well, for administrative, legal and cultural purposes, that may be so, in which case one cannot in the strictest sense talk about an expansion of the city.

I will therefore qualify my reference to the capital forthwith with the adjective 'Greater'. Indeed, the expansion of 'Greater Accra' seems to know no bounds. To the east, the area has almost caught up with Tema, the harbour city about twenty kilometres away. To the north, the borders of Nsawam, about twenty-five kilometres away, have virtually been touched. A significant expansion has also been made westwards. The little town of Kasowa, about twenty kilometres away, has in the meantime almost been engulfed by her powerful neighbour. The expansion continues to move westwards beyond Kasowa. At the rate at which the expansion is taking place, it is only a matter of time before the borders of Winneba, the coastal town about 35 kilometres away, will be reached. Only the Atlantic Ocean to the south has prevented the city from expanding in that direction!

CHAPTER 13
Spintex Road

N ot only has the city expanded phenomenally, everywhere it bubbles with frenetic economic activity. I will cite the example of the newly developed area where Lena's Inn is located to illustrate the astounding transformation the city has undergone over the last several years.

As I mentioned elsewhere, the area is generally referred to by way of the road running through it to divide it almost equally into two halves— The Spintex Road. It is reached on turning immediately to the right after emerging from under the Tetteh Quarshie Overpass heading north towards Legon.

The branch road leads first to a roundabout; the Spintex Road begins from the second exist and stretches from there over a distance of about twelve kilometres. During my last visit, not only was the road non-existent, the residential and commercial estates on either side of the road, some of them stretching a distance of more than a kilometre from the road, were also non-existent. Instead, the whole area was covered by vegetation that stretched at certain parts to the parameters of the international airport.

The immediate parameters of the Spintex Road bubble with vibrant economic activity. Just to the left of the said roundabout, a large building complex, expected to house a supermarket complex, the Accra Mall, is nearing completion.

Starting a few metres from the said roundabout, on the right side of the road, the ubiquitous street hawkers and petty traders are busily at work, looking for buyers for their wares. Over a distance of about two hundred metres, as a result of the construction work in progress on the other side of the road, these hawkers and traders have restricted their activities to the right-hand side of the road. The situation changes immediately on leaving the parameters of the construction site. From there on, the street traders have taken position on both sides of the road and remain so over a considerable distance.

All kinds of goods are on sale along the road. Whether one is looking for dining table sets, kitchen, living room furniture such as sofas, leather furniture or anything between; whether one is in search of fine quality beds and mattresses and other bedroom sets and accessories, one is sure to obtain them from traders who have taken their positions under the open skies on each side of the said road.

One may ask how those dealing in these expensive and delicate wares manage to preserve them from the hazards of the elements, particularly rain! Well, I also did wonder.

Other items on sale on both sides of the road included green plants, as well as the vases to go with them, intended to enliven the rooms of their buyers. There were also Arts and Craft articles, building materials, foodstuffs, yams, plantains, cocoyams, coconut fruits, pineapples, oranges, and even car dealers of brand new as well as used cars!

Perhaps one aspect of life along the road needs mention here. Kente, the symbol of Ashanti pride, was not only being offered for sale, but it was also being woven live by a handful of specialists in one area along the road. Perhaps, for the sake of those unfamiliar with kente, I should explain what it is!

Kente used to be a royal and sacred cloth worn only by Ashanti kings in times of extreme importance. It is woven on a narrow horizontal loom measuring about 8–12 cm in width and about 1.5 metres in length. Several strips are sewn together to make a wider piece of cloth for both men and women. (A man' s cloth may contain up to 24 strips and measure about 1.5 x 2.5 metres. The woman's two-piece cloth may contain 8–12 strips.) Over the course of time, the use of kente became more widespread. Its importance has however remained and is held in high esteem by the Akans in particular and Ghanaians in general. Bonwire, a small town in the Ashanti Region, is generally regarded as the home of kente weaving.

Kente is said to be woven at almost every corner of the town. In order probably to provide those not familiar with its production, particularly the foreign tourist, the opportunity to witness the pride of Ghana being produced, the idea occurred to someone to set up a production site along the Spintex Road.

A few days, prior to our departure, we were about to drive past the traditional weavers as usual when Rita gave me the 'order' to stop.

'I want to have a closer look at the cloths on display,' she said.

Not only did she get the opportunity to examine some of the brilliantly woven and elegant cloths at a close range, she acquired an attractive piece at a good bargain. As I waited for her I had the opportunity to quench my thirst with the juice of the coconut I bought from a teenager selling a huge pile of them nearby.

Economic activity on each side of the road was not limited to street hawking and petty trading. Several businesses including large wholesale depots dealing in all sorts of wares, shops dealing in wares ranging from washing machines, gas and electric cookers, refrigerators, deep freezers, rice, flour, etc., as well as shopping malls and grocery shops have also taken their positions on either side of the road. These businesses and shops, as I was told, are not owned only by Ghanaians, but also foreigners, including Chinese, Lebanese and Syrians.

Several banking institutions have also discovered in the expanding residential and commercial settlement a lucrative environment where the middle class of society who are increasingly moving to settle in that area could be won. Their newly constructed, elegant-looking office buildings adorn each side of the road. Among them were names previously known to me in the country—Barclays and Standard Chartered—as well as unknown ones such Cal-, Stanbic- and Zenith Banks.

Recreational facilities such as a world-class swimming pool, fast food restaurants offering pizza, chips, fried rice, grilled chicken similar to the one I mentioned earlier, ice-cafes, etc., have opened at several points along the road. The prices on display at such places are comparable with those demanded in places like Berlin, London and Paris. It is superfluous to state that on a visit there one might meet only the expatriate community, locals like ourselves on holidays from

'Aburokyire' (the term used for the West, including Europe and America) as well as the local middle-class community.

Despite its popularity (or should I rather say *due* to its popularity?) the Spintex Road has gained notoriety in one area—it is a chronically congested stretch of road! Either the city planners had not reckoned with the large expansion that the settlement that would develop alongside it would undergo or were perhaps unwilling to construct a dual carriageway through a densely populated area.

Whatever their reasons, the single tract road has, at least at the time of writing, become synonymous with traffic jams. Indeed, it has grown to the extent of becoming one of the most congested streets, if not *the* most congested street in the city. During the morning rush hour, traffic on this hopelessly congested road barely moves.

On one occasion it took me almost sixty minutes to cover the distance of about ten kilometres from the junction leading to our hotel to the end of the road towards Accra. With the previous day's experience behind me, I decided to leave home around 06:00 hrs to get something done in the city before traffic began to build up. Even then I was forced to spend considerable time in traffic that had already begun to jam at that time of day.

The authorities seem to have recognised the problem though, for just before our departure, the *Daily Graphic*, the leading national daily, carried a report concerning a demolition exercise that was carried out the previous day on a settlement bordering on one section of the road.

According to the report the authorities, in their desire to widen that section of the road, had on several occasions served eviction notices to those who had erected unauthorised structures there. As one deadline after the other expired without any sign of the residents quitting, the authorities sent bulldozers just before dawn the previous day to raze the buildings and structures to the ground.

As we drove on the road regularly on our way to and from the hotel, our attention was drawn particularly to a group of houses about half a kilometre on the right-hand side of the road. Even from a distance, the houses created the impression of belonging to a class of their own. Another observation we made concerned the quality and make of the vehicles that plied the branch road—vehicles that were far beyond the ordinary.

'That must be a place for the rich!' Rita remarked on one occasion as we drove by. A few days prior to our departure we were heading for the hotel after a visit to the city, when, instead of driving straight on, I turned right at the junction.

'You have missed the way!' the rest shouted in unison.

'I know what I am doing!'

'What are you up to then?'

'I just want to have a close look at the mansions over there.'

'Not in this dirty bus, Papa!' Karen protested. 'What will they think of us?'

'Potential robbers on a spying mission!' Rita joined in.

'Come on, we are doing nothing illegal; we are driving on a public road in a legally registered vehicle!'

As we got to the area and drove past one executive mansion after the other, I began to share the sentiments voiced by the rest of group. Affluence indeed was on display! This was reflected in the luxurious mansions lined up before us, each of them a showcase of architectural excellence. Adorning some of them were palm-lined boulevards and beautiful front gardens—a true island of the first world in a third world setting. Our *tro tro*, mercilessly stained by the mud from *Muddy Street,* was without doubt out of place in this opulent neighbourhood.

CHAPTER 14
From Turbulence to Optimism

W hat has led to the extraordinary expansion of the capital and the general improvement in economic activity that was everywhere visible? After speaking to a cross section of the population and consulting several informed sources, all were agreed on two important contributing factors: political stability and economic liberalisation. These two factors had created a favourable climate that in turn has attracted investors from all over the globe. Political stability! That has not always been associated with the little country situated on the West African coast, the country that prides itself as being the first country south of the Sahara to gain independence from colonial rule.

'We prefer independence in danger to servitude in tranquilly!' 'Independence Now!' 'The black man is capable of managing his own affairs!' With slogans like these charismatic Dr Kwame Nkrumah led the then Gold Coast to independence on 6th March 1957, renaming the newly independent country Ghana. His rule ended violently in a military coup on 24th February 1966. A military junta, the National Liberation Council (NLC), took over the reins of government.

Barely a year later, in April 1967, an unsuccessful attempt was made by another group of soldiers to oust the ruling military government. The coup plotters were tried, found guilty for treason, and executed.

In October 1969, following a general election, the NLC handed over power to the winning Progress Party (PP) led by Dr Busia. Civilian rule would last for only twenty-seven months. On January 13, 1972, a military Junta, the National Redemption Council (NRC), led by the then Col Acheampong, seized power from the civilian administration.

In July 1978, following what has been termed a palace coup, Gen Acheampong was replaced by Gen Akuffo, a ruling member of the junta. Acheampong was placed under house arrest. The name NRC was replaced with SMC (Supreme Military Council). Gen Akuffo immediately initiated plans to return the country to civilian rule.

On 4th June 1979, just as preparations for a general election was on course, a group of young army officers overthrew the ruling SMC, and Flt Lt JJ Rawlings became the new military head of state.

Within days of the take-over, eight senior military officers, including former Heads of State Gen. Acheampong and Gen. Akuffo as well as Gen. Afrifa who played a leading role in the 1966 take-over, were summarily tried and executed on various charges.

The Junta allowed the general elections to go on as planned. On 24th Sept 1979 power was duly handed over to Dr Limann of the winning PNP (Peoples National Party).

The set pattern of the military intervening to oust a civilian government to be followed by the military relinquishing power after a while only to re-grab it again, seemed to have no end, as on 31st December 1981 Rawlings seized power for a second time just as the country was settling down to civilian rule. This time he would rule for eighteen years, first as a military dictator and during the last eight years as elected president.

It is not the intention of this book to give a commentary on what happened in the country during the initial stages of Rawlings' second rule. What is generally agreed is that economic activity nearly ground to a halt towards the end of 1982.

An already precarious situation was compounded by a severe drought that gripped the country in 1982/83. This in turn favoured the spread of bushfires, some of which had been started deliberately to clear lands for cultivation. The fires swept through the country in several areas to create havoc and aggravate the misery of the population.

As if the woes plaguing the country was not enough, Nigeria expelled in 1983 at short notice several hundred thousands Ghanaians who had gone there in search of work.

It was just about that time that the terminology 'Rawlings chains' came into circulation in the country. The general lack of food in the nation had led to the emaciation of a great majority of the population.

That in turn had led to the collarbones of a considerable proportion of citizens becoming exposed. The term 'Rawlings' chains' was coined to describe the protruding collarbones.

Did it come about through a change of opinion? Was it political pragmatism in the face of harsh realities? Was it bowing to pressure from the international community? These are questions that ex-President Rawlings himself can best answer. Whatever the reason, the fact remains that Rawlings, who until then had, in his speeches, made no secret of his abhorrence of the IMF and the World Bank, made a paradigmatic U-turn and approached the IMF for a way out of the economic impasse. So was born the term Structural Adjustment Programme, or SAP for short, in Ghana. Introduced in 1983 as part of the IMF conditions for lending to the country, it led among others to the floating of the national currency, the cedi, on the international financial market which in turn led to a massive devaluation of its value; the lifting of subsidies on food, fuel and other commodities; the liberalisation of trade and exchange controls; the retrenchment of labour and a reduction in government expenditure.

Was it because the experience of 1982/83 had hardened them to the extent that they were prepared to face whatever the future had in store for them? In any case, the population somehow managed to swallow the bitter pill the SAP was forcing down their throat.

Liberalisation brought about by the SAP re-formed the state-controlled business environment and made life easier for those conducting business in Ghana. It introduced more transparency in all sectors of the economy, lifted barriers to both importing and exporting and made the formation of new foreign firms routine.

The SAP created an official channel permitting hundreds and thousands of Ghanaians in the Diaspora to transfer money home to do business or to support their family members.

Accountability was introduced into the system. Whereas in the previous times many a citizen considered the payment of electricity, water and telephone bills for example a 'voluntary act', they now faced the option of either paying or having the supply cut.

Although the SAP was introduced in 1983, it took a while for its effect to become visible. Thus during my stay in 1994, apart from being able to exchange my foreign currency without hindrance in one of the forex bureaux that had sprung up everywhere (prior to the SAP such exchange was illegal and done only underground), there was no visible sign of change in the air.

Not only did Rawlings execute a U-turn regarding how best to run the economy, he did so also in regard to how the nation should be governed. Political activity that had been outlawed since the coup of 31st December 1981 was lifted in the early nineties.

In 1992 parliamentary and presidential elections were held. At that time, the opposition boycotted the parliamentary election. Not so in 1996. Although Rawlings received a second mandate, that was to be his last tenure of office for the constitution barred presidents from running for a third time.

In the 2000 elections, instead of the charismatic Rawlings, his less flamboyant vice-President faced candidates from the opposition for the Presidency. The electorate, apparently fed up with the Rawlings era, voted the candidate of the main opposition party to power. For the first time in the turbulent political history of the country, power was transferred peacefully from one party to the other.

The favourable political and economic climate has attracted investors from all over the globe into the country. Several foreign companies have in the meantime established their presence in Accra.

As a result of the growing attractiveness of the country, well known names such as Novotel, Holiday Inn and of late Hilton Hotel have built or are planning to build in Accra.

CHAPTER 15
Absentee Homeowners

One day as I was driving with Tetteh around the hotel I drew his attention to a magnificent newly-built house not far from where we were.

'That looks gorgeous,' I began.

'It belongs to a lady resident in Canada,' he began. 'She comes to Ghana only occasionally. Indeed, a substantial proportion of the buildings around here and also in several newly developed areas of the city have been built by Ghanaians living abroad. Some build them to completion; others begin the construction work and abandon it for a while. They just do so to prevent others from encroaching on the land.'

'I have read and heard about incidents of that nature in the past; do they still happen?'

'Yes indeed, Doc! Be warned! A lot of unscrupulous persons, genuine landowners as well as fraudulent ones, have taken advantage of the high demand for building plots to cheat unsuspecting clients. They sell the piece of land to one person, only to resell the same piece to several others.

'Curiously, they, in some instances, manage to acquire the necessary paperwork for all their clients.

'There have been instances where two or more persons have clashed on the same piece of land armed with documents, which at least on face value, all appear to be genuine!

'As a way of getting around the problem, those who purchase such plots hurry to erect structures on them as a means of cementing or securing their ownership. In some instances that has turned out to be wishful thinking, when the courts have failed to recognise their claim to ownership.'

'That is bitter!'

'Well, it does happen. My personal advice to you is the following: should you decide in future to buy a house or build your own, please deal only with recognised property developers. In that situation you will know who to deal with should something go wrong. That is not always the case with individuals. There have been several reports of instances when they have just vanished into thin air.'

On the issue of Ghanaians still resident abroad putting up buildings or buying houses in Ghana, I really did not need a lecture from him. I had heard enough on the issue during the time I ran a GP practice in Duesseldorf, in Germany. The majority of my patients were Ghanaians living in the city and its surroundings.

My interaction with them taught me a lesson which I think can be regarded as typical for the majority of Ghanaians living outside the country, particularly in the West, viz: there is a general striving among the majority to put up homes back in the native country, regardless of whether such individuals have any immediate plans to settle there or not!

Does that longing derive from the fact that many of us, prior to leaving for the West, lived together with our kindred in our extended family homes, a situation we can no longer return to now that we have become conversant with the Western way of life?

Still others, including myself, grew up in the countryside, in villages some of which still lack basic amenities such as electricity, running water and proper sanitary facilities; do our critics expect us to go and settle in places like Mpintimpi and Amantia on our return?

Some have decided to plan well ahead into the future by putting up suitable homes befitting their new status.

During the period of political instability and economic restrictions at home, many persons living abroad decided to put their plans to build or buy their own homes in their native country on hold.

Things changed with the reintroduction of multiparty democracy and liberalisation of the economy. In particular, the massive devaluation of the local currency vis-à-vis other leading currencies, placed the average

Ghanaian worker in the West in a favourable position to realise their dreams of acquiring property back home.

I found it incredible, but true—a sizable proportion of my Ghanaian patients had immediate plans of either buying a home or entrusting trusted relatives or friends to do so on their behalf. Some even came to the consulting rooms with keys to their homes in Ghana or pictures of their nearly completed homes! It was astonishing, people on low wages in Germany—cleaners, kitchen and factory hands, taxi drivers—all seriously considering establishing homes back home in Ghana!

On second thought, however, I realised their dreams were not completely unrealisable. The massive devaluation of the local currency vis-a-vis other leading currencies—the dollar, euro and pound—had put them in an advantageous position; still many had to live austere lives in their bid to realise their goals.

Something else I got to learn from my patients, and which is not irrelevant as far as the massive expansion in the size of Accra is concerned—no matter from which part of the country they originally hailed from, the great majority of those I talked to were bent on establishing their houses in Accra. Kumasi, the second largest city in the country, trailed far behind in second place on their scale of preference. Even a sizeable proportion of Ashantis, the ethnic group that has Kumasi as their traditional capital, were considering building in Accra.

What happens to the homes once they are completed? Only a few consider renting them out for the reason that they would need them during their visits there, never mind if such visits take place once in a blue moon.

Renting them out is not without risk though; one could eventually end up seeing his/her property degraded by an uncaring tenant.

Some entrust their homes to selected members of the extended family. Very soon, however, the population of relatives occupying the property could begin to soar, either biologically through the caretaker or by way of other members of the extended family who initially arrive with the intention of staying on for a short period of time but eventually decide to extend their stay indefinitely.

If only things would end up there, but no! There was an occasion when one of my patients vented his anger on his extended family in

Ghana during the consultation. 'These extended family members at home!' he exploded. 'They have no idea how much we have to struggle before we earn our living here. Doc, think about it. They occupy my large property without having to pay any rent. In such a situation, one would expect them at least to pay the water and electricity bills, wouldn't one? No, they expect *me* to do that! Just as I was about to retire to bed last night they called me to inform me that their electricity had been disconnected because they had defaulted in settling their bills! Now they expect me to send them money for that purpose!'

I realised in the course of my practice that quite a lot of them had psychosomatic symptoms that were in part brought about by issues related to their dealings with their extended family members at home.

Others, probably to avoid the problems cited above, entrust their property to a group of people who used to be known as watchmen but who, as I learnt during my stay, are increasingly referred to as Security. Unlike the situation elsewhere, the security men are not supplied by an agency firm. Instead, they are often employed by way of recommendation from others. Some, perhaps only a very small minority, are not always content with having been entrusted with the care of such homes and go so far as to want to convert ownership into their own name, as the harrowing experience of one of my patients in Germany illustrated.

The caretaker she entrusted her house to managed to forge the title deeds of the house. Indeed, in the end he even managed to enter his name in appropriate quarters as the rightful owner of the property.

It was only after several involuntary trips to Ghana to face the impostor in court that she was finally recognised as the rightful owner.

CHAPTER 16
Helping By Proxy

While not underestimating the contribution foreign investment has made towards the economic revival of the country, one cannot fail to acknowledge the enormous contribution made by one group of people, namely the so-called Ghanaians in the Diaspora.

The remarkable expansion in the size of Accra referred to above is largely due to the homes that have either been built or bought by this group of people. The Ghanaians in the Diaspora have played a vital role in the economic turn around, not only in regard to the building sector but also by way of direct investment. They have also helped ward off a possible social upheaval that could have resulted from the suffering brought about by the radical measures associated with the SAP.

Laying off several public service workers to curtail public sector spending without any benefit system as is found in the welfare states of Western Europe might have led to a social rebellion. How indeed would a father, a person who spent much of his life producing cocoa beans to support the national economy and who has no pension to fall back on in his old age, for example, have survived the harsh economic realities brought about by the SAP without the support from his children abroad? The same thing applies to millions of others.

With over two million of its citizens overseas, in the EU, USA, Canada, South Africa etc., remittance flowing into Ghana is of major significance to the country's economy.,

President Kufuor was recently quoted as saying that between 2001 and 2006, approximately US$7–8 billion was remitted into Ghana by Ghanaians in the Diaspora.

Already, official figures for the year 2007 indicate that remittances in the first quarter of the year hit US$ 2 billion.

The Bank of Ghana has estimated that remittances by Ghanaians abroad make up about 15% of the country's GDP. There has been public debate in recent years as to whether Ghana's model could be copied by other developing countries. When it comes to the matter of democracy, human rights, freedom of the press, my response is an unequivocal yes.

While not being an authority in matters of Economics, Financing and Banking, my instinct tells me that in a poor country whose citizens do not have a bonus of a large Diaspora population such as in the case of Ghana who are prepared to remit liberally to support relatives at home, a less radical economic restructuring should be attempted.

I am aware that what I am about to suggest is not likely to gain a working majority in appropriate quarters. Still, as far as I am concerned, serious thought should be given to the idea of lending money to the very poor countries of this world on an interest free basis.

Expecting desperately impoverished country X, a country whose economy is not only in shambles but threatened with near collapse to pay even a percentage point interest on a loan granted by country Y swimming in absolute wealth amounts, in my opinion, to a scandal. Accepted, some of the leaders of such countries make a precarious situation even worse through corruption. They too should be held to account.

CHAPTER 17
Oprah's Soulmate

A nother sign of the breeze of freedom blowing all over the country is the proliferation of the media that operates freely with no notable constraint on its right and freedom of expression.

Thirteen years ago the state controlled the media. The state-owned GBC (Ghana Broadcasting Corporation) was centralised in Accra and boasted only a couple of channels.

The state of affairs was utilised by the coup planners. They only needed to take control of the buildings of the GBC to get access to the whole nation by way of Radio.

The situation changed when the country returned to civilian rule in 1992. The state gradually loosened control over the media, thus giving way to a rapidly evolving private media scene. Today, there are about forty local newspapers and twenty magazines and tabloids available.

The number of FM radio stations in the country has in the meantime risen to over sixty. The inventiveness (or shall we say fantasies?) of their owners seems to know no bounds in their search for names for their stations—PEACE-, JOY-, MERCURY-, GOLD-FM, etc.

The public TV channel has been joined by five private TV stations in Accra and Kumasi, as well as a number of cable television providers. Another sign of the self-confidence sweeping the country is this: in former times, English, the language of the ex-colonial master, Britain, dominated affairs in Radio and also TV—but no longer.

Now Twi, the language spoken by the majority of the population, is offering English a real challenge.

It isn't Twi alone that is spoken freely on Radio and TV these days; other local languages—Ga, Ewe, Dagbani, etc., are also well represented. The impression I gained was that the tendency these days is to allow anyone who has something to tell the world by way of Radio or TV the opportunity to do so in the language familiar to him or her instead of resorting to the English language[3].

In former times, the way programmes were run on Radio might as well be described as a one-way street with the presenter or moderator speaking to an anonymous audience. That is no longer the case. Thanks to the widespread use of mobile phones, listeners are now enabled to phone in to a live broadcast and ask questions or take part in a discussion.

The topic that dominated the public debate was the issue that had been dubbed the ENERGY CRISIS. Even before our visit, I had been following the matter on the Internet. It involved the rationalisation of electricity in the country. This had been brought about, so the official version went, by the falling levels of the Volta River on which the dam that supplies the hydro-electric power station at Akosombo, about 150 kilometres to the north-east of Accra, had been built.

Since August of the previous year the country had been plagued by regular power outages. This in turn led to a boom in one area of economic activity—the sale of electric generators both for domestic and commercial use. Whereas there seemed to be a general consensus regarding the adverse effects of the frequent power cuts on the consumer and the economy at large, there was no agreement on the factor(s) that had led to the situation.

The official version was that the rationalisation had been necessitated by falling water levels of the Akosombo dam. Constructed about 40 years ago, it has faithfully supplied electricity not only for homes, hospitals, and schools, but also to run machines in factories and other industrial estates.

---

[3] Ghana has several languages, many of which have no relationship with one another, just like English has little or no similarity to Russian. Twi, however, is spoken and understood by the majority. Twi, however, is spoken and understood by the majority.

In former times the country could not utilise all the energy generated; the surplus was exported to some of the neighbouring countries. As to be expected, the opposition parties sought to gain political capital from the situation, as they accused the government of incompetence in handling the situation and promised the populace to reverse the situation in the shortest possible time should they be voted into power.

The debate was not left to the politicians alone. One day as we waited in our *tro-tro* at Nkawkaw for Rita who had gone to purchase some items to return, I followed a lively discussion on the local FM station on the energy crisis.

'I am of the opinion that the government is not telling us all the truth on the matter,' one caller asserted.

'So what do you think has led to the situation?' the presenter inquired.

'Lack of maintenance, simply lack of maintenance! We Africans have the tendency not to maintain things once they have been acquired. The Akosombo dam was built by President Nkrumah over forty years ago, right? At that time I myself was nowhere in this world. Now tell me how often has the dam been serviced? Fact is, one government after the other came and went without thinking of overhauling it. Indeed, that should have happened twenty years ago. Now we are paying the price of that neglect!'

'But the government is telling us that the problem is due to the low water level; and that in turn has been brought about by the lack of rainfall in recent years!' the presenter came in.

'What do you mean by lack of rains?'

'That is what the government is saying. They say it has not been raining of late.'

'Do you believe them? Believe me, just as I am talking to you, there is flooding in our area—the result of the torrential rains of recent days. Indeed, only yesterday we had a heavy downpour here.'

'It may be raining in your area, but that will have no effect on the water level of the dam. The rain should pour in the area where the rivers supplying the dam flow.'

'Well, I agree with you on that point; still, I suspect a cover-up is going on somewhere.'

Hardly had that caller hung up, than another phoned in.

'Why is the government incapable of telling the population the bare truth?' he began.

'What do you mean by that?'

'The problem has nothing to do with the falling water levels. Rather, it is the result of the enormous strain on the national grid. I am for example calling from a small town. Ten years ago, no one here dreamt of electricity. Then came the National Electrification Program aimed at extending electricity to several areas in the country. The laudable program was executed without taking into account the supply side by building additional sources of supplies to supplement the Akososmbo station. Now demand has overrun supply. Lack of foresight on the side of our leaders has brought us into this situation.'

At that stage the presenter asked callers to suspend all calls while he played some music in a musical interlude.

The discussion continued after the interlude.

'Don't blame the government for our predicament. Rather, let us put the blame squarely on our own shoulders. Yes, in my opinion the energy crisis is due to sin and evil that is widespread in our country. My goodness, how much has evil spread in our country! The falling water level is God's retribution on our nation for turning our backs on the Almighty! It is a clarion call for repentance!

Yes, there is the need for national repentance, failing which the Almighty Father will unleash an even more terrible catastrophe on us.'

Just as he hung up, another listener called.

'I totally disagree with the last caller regarding that extraordinary assertion! That is indeed ridiculous! Let us consider a country like the USA, friends! The USA, as far as I am concerned, is the headquarters of evil in the whole world. Following his line of thinking, the US should also be experiencing power outages. That, however, is not the case. Friends, it is time we learnt to fix our problems on our own rather than look up to supernatural powers to fix them for us or apportion blame to them for whatever goes wrong in our lives in our society!'

Rita in the meantime had returned and we had to continue our journey. I would have liked to follow the discussion further. Unfortunately, since the antenna on our *tro-tro* was broken, the reception was not good enough and soon we were out of range of the transmission.

I could only congratulate my countrymen and women on their newfound freedom. Several years ago, such an open discussion, a discussion that bordered on criticising the ruling government, would have been unheard of.

The proliferation of the media is also evident in the area of Television. The public TV channel has been joined by several (five) private TV stations in Accra and Kumasi as well as a number of cable television providers. We got a taste of this the very first day of our stay. There was a TV in each of our rooms. It was Karen who first switched it on, shortly after we had settled down. Thirteen years before she would have been disappointed for there would be nothing to view at that time of day. GBC-TV, the only channel available, began operation in the late afternoon and ended transmission around midnight. As mentioned above, there was no alternative channel to switch to—one either watched what GBC-TV offered or switched the set off.

Now there were several channels to choose from—one could either follow world events on CNN, view national news and events on GTV, watch a TV-Evangelist preach his/her own versions of the Gospel of Christ or a live Talk Show on Metro TV or be thrilled by Reality TV in action on TV 3.

A few days after our arrival Karen, armed with the remote control, was switching from one station to another, when suddenly her mother shouted:

'Stop for a moment! I want to find out what Maame Dokono is up to.'

Yes indeed, on the screen was the popular Ghanaian actress, known also by her original name Grace Omaboe. The name Maame Dokono has in the meantime become a household word in Ghana. She first entered the limelight in the 1980s when she featured in a popular Ghanaian soap opera. Since then she has been active in various spheres of life—as actress, social worker as well as social commentator in Radio and TV.

As we were soon to discover, she has in the meantime also gained popularity as Talkmistress in a show captioned in Twi—*Odo ne asomdwee* (Love and Peace). She is said to combine so many qualities akin to Oprah Winfrey that she is in the meantime generally regarded as the Ghana equivalent of the internationally renowned TV-Talkmistress.

It did not take long for us to grasp what the talk for the evening was about, for the cameras were soon focussed on a horribly disfigured young woman aged about twenty, seated not far from the renowned personality.

'No, please, no—switch to another station!' Jonathan screamed. 'I cannot bear to see that horrifying figure.'

'Turn your attention to something else if you cannot bear it,' his sister objected. 'I am curious to learn what led to that situation!'

'No, I do not want to view it!'

'Why should we allow the wish of the youngest member of the group to override that of everyone else!'

In the end the vote of the majority prevailed. The loser was left with no other choice than to turn his attention away from the TV whenever the afflicted lady appeared on the screen.

'How come any human being can be capable of inflicting such a horrible act on a fellow human being?' the Talkmaster began in a compassionate, caring, motherly manner. 'Anyone watching, please listen carefully—should you happen to have any information that can lead to the arrest of the young man involved please call the number on the screen or go to the nearest police station and make a report. He has to account for this ugly crime—pouring acid on this woman, and for the only reason she turned down his marriage proposal. It is incomprehensible, simply incomprehensible …'

Further details came to light in the course of the program. The victim was said to be the queen of her community. Those conversant with the Akan tradition would appreciate the honour, respect and authority associated with her position. It is a title that is conferred not by virtue of one being married to the chief or king. Instead, it is inherited by virtue of belonging to the extended family, the members of which are custodians of the land of the community. The queen of an Akan community thus usually bears a direct blood relationship to the chief or king of that area.

A picture of the victim before the incident was displayed on the screen during the show, showing an attractive, compassionate-looking young woman bubbling with vigour. Did she in the end fall victim to her noble looks and position? As it was revealed, the culprit was her former boyfriend. In the course of time he proposed marriage to her. The queen, not prepared to marry, turned down the proposal. Disappointed at the turn of events, he hatched his evil plan. On the pretext of talking matters over with her, he invited her to a meeting. Unsuspecting, she turned up for the meeting. Then it all happened, and very quickly—he poured the acid over her from a container he had concealed on his person.

The attack led to complete blindness in one eye and a severely impaired vision in the other. Indeed, one of her eyeballs had almost completely dissolved in its socket through the action of the aggressive liquid! The skin on her whole face had turned into scars and keloids. Due to the scarring of her facial muscles, she could hardly close her mouth, as a result of which her speech was severely impeded. The left side of her body bore the brunt of the attack. The left arm was permanently flexed at the elbow due to the scarring of muscles there. One could only guess at the extent of damaged skin the clothes she wore concealed.

The program was meant not only to help capture the offender who had been at large since the incident happened two years before, but also to raise funds to help the victim undergo plastic surgery.

'Help us, businessmen, help us, chief executives, help us, pastors, help us—whoever can—by donating generously towards this noble cause!' Thus Maame Dokona appealed to her viewers. One could easily read the anguish in her face.

Her appeal for information leading to the arrest of the offender was not in vain, for a few days after the program the cold-hearted assailant was reported to have been arrested.

Reality TV of some kind has also found its way to Ghana. As I observed, most of the shows are sponsored by the mobile phone companies—not without their own interest in mind, of course! As has become customary in other parts of the world, in Ghana, too, the viewers of such shows were given the opportunity to vote for their favourites by means of the phone. Since mobile phones are more widespread in comparison to landlines, it is not surprising that the mobile phone companies pay to get the shows going. Welcome to the free capitalistic market, Ghana!

The World Wide Web has also made significant inroads in the country. I came across Internet cafes in almost every city and big town we visited. The speed at which information was transmitted by some of

93

them was too slow for my liking, however. Never mind! The important thing is that they were functioning. With some patience I had the opportunity, for example, to book working sessions with my agency in the UK and also exchange e-mails with relatives and friends in Europe and the USA. Welcome to the global village, Ghana.

CHAPTER 18
The Talking Handkerchiefs

A lmost everyone above the age of about eighteen years that I saw on the streets of Accra and elsewhere seemed to be in possession of a mobile phone! Alberta, the wife of Junior, did not exaggerate when she told me in a conversation that mobile phones have become something like handkerchiefs to Ghanaians.

The spread of mobile usage in the country is indeed phenomenal. I recently read a report on the Internet which quoted the country's Communications Minister as saying that the country's subscriber base for mobile phones and fixed lines had grown from a mere 400,000 in 2001 to 6 million by July 24, 2007! Mobile phone subscribing no doubt forms the bulk of the figure, for whereas landlines are still not available in several areas of the countryside, mobile phone signals could be received almost everywhere I visited in the country.

As a result of the widespread use of mobile phones in the country one scene has become common on the streets—that of vendors sitting in small kiosks, in makeshift wooden structures and also on chairs placed behind tables along the roadside, offering SIM-cards and top-up units for sale.

Mobile phone use is not only popular with city and urban dwellers but also with the rural population. Indeed, as I observed during my visit to Mpintimpi, the gadgets have been popular with those residing in the countryside.

Kofi Ampomah, my half-brother who, after his elementary education chose to remain in the village to engage in farming, seemed to be an exception to the rule.

'Why don't you possess your own mobile phone?' I inquired.

'Bro (short for brother), I always thought the phones were meant for those who really need them, like businessmen and women to facilitate communication with their clients, not for some of the residents I meet on the streets here who display their devices for the whole world to see. Some of them hardly use their cell phones. To them it is just fashionable to possess the devices, so they are prepared to stretch their resources to acquire them simply to let the whole world know they are up to date with the latest trends in town. You know one funny thing regarding some of those walking about with mobile phones here? Once they have acquired them, some of them hardly find the means to top-up their credits. After a while they are disconnected. The gadgets then become what I would describe as monuments in their pockets! I have decided not to follow the crowd blindly. I prefer to invest my resources in the education of my children rather than in something I do not need.'

Regarding the difficulty many a mobile phone user in the country has in maintaining sufficient credit on their phones, I had in the meantime made my own discovery. As I mentioned earlier on, we bought two SIM cards shortly on our arrival. In due course, relatives and friends got to know our number. Soon something that was unusual to me began to happen to my phone! It would begin to ring; I would rush to pick it up, only to find it had ceased to ring—barely after the first ring! After that had happened a couple of times, I voiced my exasperation.

'What in the world is going on with my phone!' I cried out.

'Nothing is wrong, Doc,' Joyce calmed me down. 'You are only being flashed by someone!'

'Flashed? What is that?'

'Doc! You must know what is meant by the terminology by now! You have definitely been using the mobile phone for a while!'

'You must excuse your outmoded uncle for not being up to date with all aspects of this modern technology,' I smiled.

'Well, flashing is when I call your number and hang-up before you pick it up! Over here in Ghana it is generally resorted to for monetary considerations. Many people, and I am no exception, are not always in a position to top up their phones regularly. I usually keep enough units on my phone to allow for a connection. I will wait for the phone on the other side to ring once and then hang-up, expecting the other person to call back!'

'What happens if he or she does not?'

'I keep on trying.'

'What would happen should every mobile user resort to flashing?'

'Well, I am just describing the situation as it is here: it is a situation borne out of poverty. One should not underestimate the important role being played by mobile phones in the country, however.'

'I do agree with you on that point. I remember as I was growing up at Mpintimpi, we were always scared when we saw Kwadwo Boye, our relative living in Amantia, about fifty kilometres away, approaching our home. He was the person usually sent by members of the extended family there to carry important messages to us. Eventually we bestowed on him the title "harbinger of bad news" for he was usually sent on such errands when either a member of the extended family there was seriously ill or had passed away. In the course of time, whenever we saw him approaching our home, mother would meet him with the words: "Kwadwo, please allow us time to enjoy our dinner before you break your distressing news." In this age of mobile phones, such errands would be superfluous. The mobile phone makes one terribly accessible, wherever one is, and whatever the time of day.'

CHAPTER 19
Wild Rats for Dinner

Ten days after our arrival it was finally time to leave Accra for the countryside. Apart from the joy of re-union with our respective family members, the thought of leaving congested Accra, at least for a while, was comforting.

We checked out of our hotel, packed all our belongings into our bus and set off. Our first destination was Mpintimpi, the village where my eyes first saw the light of day and where I grew up. Father, who was now in his eighties, as well as my younger sister, Manu, and several other close relatives, are still resident there.

Owing to the unavailability of accommodation suitable for the children, we would stay at a hotel at Nkawkaw, about thirty kilometres away, which Kwasi, at our request, had booked for us. Nkawkaw is about 130 kilometres to the north of Accra and lies on the main road leading from Accra to Kumasi.

In former days, the journey from Accra to Nsawam, the next major town on our route, a distance of about twenty kilometres, could be reached in about half an hour.

Not so on this occasion. As I would soon discover, not only had the capital almost grown to the outskirts of its northern neighbour, the volume of traffic between the two towns had also grown considerably. In the end it took us about double the time I originally thought we would require for that part of the journey.

As we drove a few kilometres beyond Nsawam, however, I was struck by the fact that the road we were travelling on as well as the towns and villages we drove through seemed in comparison to my previous visits to be deserted. The difference became even more striking the further we drove from Accra.

My observation was confirmed later in my conversations with several residents. Indeed, quite a good proportion of the rural population has indeed migrated to Accra in particular and to some extent Kumasi in search of work, leaving the countryside fairly deserted.

It was in the rainy season. The rains seemed to have fallen in the recent past. This was reflected in the blooming and blossoming of green vegetation on each side of the road. Just as I was enjoying the scenery, Rita, who was seated a little distance behind me, cried suddenly: 'That is a rat for sale!'

Just then I took note of what she was drawing my attention to. Standing by the roadside with a raised right arm was a young man whose age I put at about twenty. He held on to a large Gambian pouched rat that, judging from his gesture, was for sale.

'Let's go for it!' she exclaimed.

'What, for goodness sake, do you want to do with a rat?' Karen asked, surprised

'Prepare a good meal! What else do you expect?'

'Disgusting! The thought of it makes me feel sick!'

'Rat for a meal … eeehhhhhhhh!' Jonathan, who had taken a seat beside me, yelled.

'That is good meat, I tell you,' I remarked.

As we drove past the young man, my thoughts went back to the days when I was growing up at Mpintimpi. It was our habit—my brothers and I, and some of our peers—to go hunting for the long-tailed rodents. The rodents usually dwell in burrows inside hillocks. They usually rest during the day and go out at night under the cover of darkness in search of food. We used to insert long lean branches of plants growing in the area into holes leading from the outside into the bellies of the hillocks or knolls so as to disturb their rest and, in so doing, force them out of their safe abode into the open. In the meantime the rest of the group, including in some case a dog or dogs, had taken positions at strategic points on the hillock. Sometimes one of us managed to kill them just as they came out into the open. At other times they managed to escape our initial attempt to hunt them. We would then give chase in hot pursuit. We were not always successful, though—at least, from our point of view!

The rest of the journey to Nkawkaw was uneventful. We checked in at our hotel at around 1600 hrs. We decided against continuing our journey to Mpintimpi that day because the children were exhausted and also because we wanted to avoid having to travel in the dark. Anyone who has lived in the tropics knows that there is an abrupt transition from light to darkness around 1800 hrs.

CHAPTER 20
The Threat of Financial Suicide

꒰꒷꒦꒷꒰

I t was around midday the next day when we set out on our journey to Mpintimpi. It was the first time I had visited there since 1991. During our visit in 1994, we decided against travelling there mainly because we were hard-pressed with time and also due to the fact that practically the whole village had turned up at Amantia to be part of mother's funeral ceremony.

As we drew near to the village, emotions began to overflow in my heart. That little settlement will always have a special place in my heart, not only for having been the place where I was born, but also for having contributed to the formation of my character. The impoverished environment taught me, among other things, how to live with want, how to share with others to survive and, most importantly, how to believe in God, the provider of all things to survive in situations of desperate need.

I was proud to show my three children who, through Providence, were born into a totally different environment, the place where my umbilical cord is buried, and from where I rose to my present situation. Would they, after their visit there, learn to be content with what they have been blessed with?

After about forty-five minutes' drive on a road that, despite having been tarred only a few years earlier, was riddled with potholes in several areas, we finally got to the outskirts of the village.

Formerly the road leading from Nkawkaw to Akim Oda passed through the centre of the village. The newly constructed road linking both towns no longer does that, and instead passes by close to the outskirts of the village. What used to be the main road has now become a branch road leading from the new road to the village. It does not end there, however. Amenam, a village about ten kilometres to the southwest, is still reached only by the old road.

As we got to the outskirts of the village, I pointed out to the children what used to be our home on the left side of the road. It was easy to direct strangers to it, because it was the first house on the left heading from Nkawkaw to Akim Oda. I knew that Manu, mother's only child remaining in the village, had moved to a small house she had managed to put up with her own resources. Our former home had been entrusted to a peasant family that had in the meantime moved into the village to till the land.

I realised as we drove past that the roof was partly damaged. What had happened to it, I wondered? For the children's benefit I pointed to Father's extended family house, just in the middle of the village, to the left. That was where he lived the greater part of his life, until he moved to a new one my brother Ransford had built for him two years before. I had been told of its approximate location— about two hundred metres from the old one in the same direction we were travelling in, also to the left.

A handful of the villagers had gathered in and around a wooden structure serving as a shop, not far from the extended family house. I looked out for a familiar face—I could find none. Sadly, I had become a stranger in the village of my birth. Still confident I could make out Father's new home without help, I failed to stop to ask for assistance. I was so preoccupied looking for Father's new home that I had forgotten that Mpintimpi was a village that stretched barely five hundred metres from one end to the other.

'Papa, we are surely nearing the other end of your village! Ahead of us I can see no more buildings—just thick bush.' Karen was indeed right. Though the village has in the meantime extended some distance beyond its original boundary, we were just about to drive beyond it.

'Well, we have no choice but to turn back,' I told them.

At the spot where we had come to a halt the vegetation reached to the edges of the road, a difficult if not an impossible place to conduct a reverse manoeuvre. I drove slowly in the hope of finding a suitable place to swing round. Soon we came to a spot I deemed fit for the purpose.

'So you really did grow up in this little village?' Karen asked, just as I found the reverse gear.

'Young girl, did I tell you anything else? You can thank God for what you are!' I sought and found the reverse gear. Soon the manoeuvre was underway. After I had reversed a short distance, I attempted to move forward and turn towards the direction we had come from. To my dismay, instead of moving forward, the vehicle remained stationary. I pressed the accelerator once, twice, three times— the front wheels seemed willing to move but not the rear ones! Try as I might, the vehicle just wouldn't budge! The loud noise emanating from the diesel engine was in the meantime quite deafening.

After a while I got out to find out what was wrong. What I feared was confirmed— both rear wheels, especially the one on the left, had almost completely sunk into thick, slippery mud! There was no way we were going to get out of there on our own.

The frustration in the eyes of all the occupants of the vehicle was clearly evident. We had come all the way from Accra just to get stuck, and just as we were almost at our destination!

That brought home memories of an incident that happened during my last visit to the village.

I was on what was intended to be a complete surprise visit there. Not only had I kept my journey to the country a secret from the villagers, they were also unaware that I had arrived in the country a week earlier, and also that I was visiting the village on that day.

About half a kilometre away, and with the village in full view, the wheels of the vehicle spun on the gravelled untarred road. In the process, I lost control of the vehicle and watched helplessly as it strayed from the road and crashed into a ditch by the roadside!

The noise of the impact was so loud that it could be heard in the village. Some even saw the accident happening! Soon the whole village was rushing to the scene of the accident, unsuspecting that the person they thought was in faraway Germany was involved. One can imagine the shock on their faces on seeing me!

I had escaped unhurt. Not so the young man of about twenty-five who sat beside me. About twenty minutes prior to the crash I had given him a lift. He was on his way to Afosu, a town about seven kilometres away from Mpintimpi. His hope was that on getting to Mpintimpi he could find another vehicle to take him to his destination, or when that was not forthcoming, walk the remaining distance. He suffered a severe bruise to his left knee, which needed to be treated in hospital.

Since he did not have the means to do so, I gave him sufficient money to enable him to do that. As I learnt later, an X-ray did not reveal any fracture. Concerning the car we were travelling in, given to me by Ransford, apart from two completely damaged wheels, it also escaped unscathed.

In the meantime—coming back to the present!—the attention of some of the residents in the surrounding buildings had been drawn to our plight. Was it out of curiosity? Was it out of a desire to offer assistance? Whatever the reason, several of them headed towards us. Before long some of them recognised me.

'Peprah oooh! Peprah oooh!! Peprah oooh!' they screamed in unison and rushed towards us.

Soon I saw Manu emerge from a house not far from where we were. On seeing us she ran to embrace me, shouting my name at the top of her voice. The delight on seeing me again after more than a decade was clearly evident. Though we had notified her about our visit that day, we had been vague regarding the precise arrival time.

'Hurry up into the centre of the village and tell any young man you meet there what has happened. We need their assistance.' She gave this instruction to a young lad in the group.

A short while later several young men of the village hurried to our aid. After about fifteen minutes' concerted effort from about half a dozen well-built young men, the vehicle was freed from the mud. Father was clearly delighted to see us. Kofi Gyamfi! He can without doubt count himself as blessed. Born somewhere around 1922 (exact date is unknown), he has managed to make it to approximately 85 years, and that in spite of the harsh living conditions he is exposed to daily.

Not only can he count himself blessed by virtue of his advanced age; he is also one of the most respected residents of the village. Furthermore, he had no fear of becoming isolated from the mainstream of society, as is the lot of many a person of his age, particularly those living in the highly industrialised but individualised West. On the contrary, he can always count on the company of someone, either from among his numerous direct descendants, children, grandchildren, great grand children and also from members of his extended family, as the case may be. It was a great reunion—in Father's case, not after almost thirteen years, but rather after barely four. That was when we saw him off after his trip to Düsseldorf in Germany in 2003, following our invitation to visit. Since then, according to news reaching us, he had not ceased to use any opportunity to lecture the villagers about his experience in the land of Akwasi Buroni, the European!

Our reunion followed the usual ritual demanded by our tradition when someone calls for a visit. Those who follow it to the letter go through it irrespective of the time that has elapsed between the two meetings—a day, days, weeks, months or years.

First, the host offers the guest something to drink. Tradition demands that it should be water, although some these days serve any kind of drink. Thereafter, the host asks the guest to explain the reason for his or her coming, even if, as in our case, it is clearly self-evident. Finally, the host tells the guest 'what has been burning' in his or her back yard of late.

At our request the first part of the rite was skipped (we had resolved to drink only bottled water and had enough to last us for several days). Next we were asked to give the reason for our coming. I decided to be brief and precise. Since the passing away of mother in 1994, we had not been able to make it to Ghana. He was our guest in Germany in 2003. In the meantime we had moved to the UK. The opportunity had at last presented itself. So in short we were there on a short visit.

Now it was the turn of the host to tell us what had transpired there since my last visit. Tradition has it that the elderly and respected members of the community do not have to narrate such matters on their own, but rather with the help of an Okyeame (Spokesperson).

Kofi Ampomah, my half-brother, who acted as Okyeame, was also brief. I had last been seen in 1994. In 2003 the old man was in Germany. He had spoken much about his visit. Rumours had in the meantime begun to circulate to the effect that I was in the country. Everyone was delighted that at long last I had been able to visit.

In the meanwhile more than twenty residents of the village—relatives close and distant, old friends and acquaintances, as well as those I did not know—had gathered in and around the compound of Father's new home to welcome one of their own back into their midst.

The presence of some of my former close associates of the little settlement led me to recall memories of my life in the village. As I, in those days, walked with some of those assembled to attend the elementary school at Nyafoman, three kilometres away, did I ever imagine that I would one day be what I am?

As far as I was concerned, all the glory and honour belongs to the Lord Jesus Christ to whom alone I attributed my rise from nowhere to my present status. As we enjoyed the company of those assembled, someone drew our attention to an unusual spectacle—Jonathan was busy at work chasing a poor little lamb all over the place!

Almost all eyes were directed towards him.

'What is he up to?' I could hear some scream.

'Doc, don't you have such beings in Aburokyire?' one of them wanted to know.

'Yes, indeed, there are.'

'Why then is he behaving as if this were the first time he has seen them?'

'Well, over in the UK and elsewhere in the West such animals are usually kept on farmsteads. They are not allowed to roam freely on streets, to mingle with humans, or pedestrians, the way it sometimes happens here.'

'Is that indeed the case?'

'Yes; over there, one dares not leave one's animals to roam about on the streets looking for food and causing havoc in the gardens of neighbours.'

'You must be living on a different planet! I do not need to tell you how things are here. These creatures are often a nuisance to others. I tried to grow vegetables in my garden. No sooner had the plants begun to spring up than goats and sheep poured in from all over the place to destroy them. In the end I had to put up a fence to save the situation.'

So began what turned out to be the favourite sport of the youngest member of our group—*animal chasing*, as we christened it! Indeed, wherever we visited—Mpintimpi, Mim, Amantia—Jonathan would occupy himself chasing sheep, goats, cats, chickens and in some cases even dogs. We warned him to be careful concerning mother fowls on outings with their young for they had a tendency to fight back—when they perceive a threat to their young ones.

The young boy didn't seem to take our warnings seriously and chose to do exactly what we had warned him against. This led on a few occasions to a role reversal, as he was often forced to run for his life in the face of a furious mother-hen clearly not amused by the antics of this naughty boy from Europe on an African tour.

In our society custom demands that he/she who returns to a village after being away for a considerable period of time goes through the whole settlement, house to house, to greet the residents. For practical reasons the tradition is not adhered to strictly in large settlements. Not so in the case of a village like Mpintimpi.

He who neglects the tradition could reckon with the complaints of the residents should they happen to come in contact with them. To avoid such a situation, I decided to fulfil that social obligation after we had rested for a while.

At my request, Kofi Ampomah accompanied us. Having been away for such a long period of time, I thought he would be of help not only in introducing me to the inhabitants of the homes we were to visit, but also to help me become acquainted with them.

The first place of call was the building just next to that of Father's in the direction we had come from. It used to be the home of my paternal grandmother, and is where she used to live with her several children. Grandfather on his part, lived in his extended family home several metres away.

As Kofi told me, only father's eldest sister Auntie Afia Mera was still living there, the rest having either moved from the village or having moved to the homes they have built for themselves. It used to be a large round building built of bricks and boasted several rooms where grandmother lived with her several children.

As in the case of several other buildings in the village, it was roofed by means of corrugated aluminium sheets. The open compound of the building was used for cooking. When I was young it was counted among the most prominent buildings in the community.

As we approached it, I was astonished to find that not only was the roofing torn apart in several places but also that almost half of the building itself had collapsed to the ground.

'What happened, Kofi?' I inquired.

'I thought you heard about it!'

'About what?

'The tornado that hit the village a few weeks ago! It caused considerable damage to the buildings in the village. Indeed more than half of the buildings were affected—some had their roofs torn away, some saw their walls collapsing, others were completely razed to the ground.'

Just then I recalled the telephone conversation I had with Thomas, my brother resident in Amsterdam a few weeks prior to our departure for Ghana, a conversation in which he spoke about a severe storm that had hit the village and that had caused considerable damage to property. Never did I imagine at that time the extent of the damage caused.

I was lost for words. Life can indeed at times be ruthless, I thought. Indeed, if there was any group of people on the planet who could least afford such a mishap, it was the impoverished citizens of Mpintimpi.

Auntie noticed the surprise on my face. 'Well, that is what we have been made to go through. We are dying of poverty—and then this!'

'Did you receive help from any quarter to help you rebuild?'

'What help!' Kofi retorted. 'We indeed informed the NADMO. Instead of sending substantial help they only despatched a handful of blankets.'

'What do you mean by NADMO, Kofi?'

'Oh, I forgot that you have been away for such a long time! Well, it is known as National Disaster Management Organisation.'

'Do we in the meantime have a national relief agency?'

'Yes, indeed. It was established by the government several years ago. But as our example tells you, there is little substance behind the big name!'

'Still, it is a sign of progress, I suppose. At least now one has a body to appeal to in times of disaster.'

'Kofi,' Auntie Afia, now in her late seventies, began, addressing me by my first name, 'our main problem is poverty, poverty, and once more, poverty. There are times when I have barely anything to live on. Now that you are visiting, I trust you are going to provide me with the means that will be enough to sustain me for the rest of my life!'

'I will do what I can to help,' I replied. From there we moved on to the next house, the family home where father's grandmother used to live. It differed little from the one we had just visited. Father moved there from the time he was about twenty and remained there until he moved into his present home.

'This is where I now have my sleeping room,' Kofi began just as we were about to enter the gate of the main building. 'I spend the day in a small hut I have built at the other end of the village with my wife and the children. It serves as our kitchen. In the evening we come over here to sleep.'

Just then it occurred to me that in contrast to the building we had just visited, the one we were entering was fully intact with no sign of damage to it.

'Your sleeping room got off scot-free, Kofi!' I exclaimed.

'Amazing, isn't it? It was a real answer to prayer. I happened to be here when it all began. The whole building began to shake. It was brief but terrifying. What was to be done? Nothing but pray, I said to myself. So I put my feet firmly to the ground and fervently prayed to God to spare us from disaster. As you can see for yourself, my prayer was answered—the violent windstorm passed over, leaving the building unscathed.'

From there we moved on to the neighbouring homes, shaking one hand after the other as we went. Kofi had to do a lot of introduction. As far as residents below the age of twenty were concerned, I was a mere phantom, the big Uncle of the village who had made it to Aburokyire.

On my part, I could hardly separate a relative from a stranger among the several new faces on the street.

Finally we came to the place I was all along longing to show to the family, the place where my umbilical cord is buried, the place where I spent the most part of my first twenty years on earth. As might be expected, my emotions began to boil in me as we approached the humble dwelling!

I noticed, as we approached the village, that the tornado had not spared this building. Almost half of the two-room brick building, the part that served as sleeping room for mother and the three sisters, had collapsed. The corrugated aluminium roof covering that part of the building had also been ripped off. I was surprised no one had informed me about the damage.

'This house needs to be restored,' I said emphatically. 'We should not leave it to waste away!'

'He wants to keep it as a monument to the memory of the most famous resident of the village,' Rita remarked sarcastically.

'Whatever the reason, I will do my best to have it restored.'

'Well, if you can come up with about five million cedis, it could be brought back to its former shape.'

'Keep me reminded so that I do not forget,' I said. 'I expect to be bombarded with so many requests for help that this one might easily slip my memory.'

As we continued on our rounds, one thing struck me—it was not only Accra that was expanding, even little Mpintimpi had grown considerably in size since my last visit.

'Despite all your problems you are still managing to put up homes, Kofi!'

'Well, we are managing, Doc! There is the tendency these days for people to move away from the big extended family home, to put up their own homes, even if they are humble ones. Manu our sister has done it, Kwaku Driver, our cousin, has done it, Ama Alice, our niece, has as well.'

'That marks a significant development.'

'Indeed. No one wants to break links with the extended family; nevertheless the generation of today seems to yearn for a certain degree of independence and some privacy from the all-intruding eyes of extended family members.'

In yet other significant ways the Mpintimpi I was visiting had been transformed from the Mpintimpi I was accustomed to. By virtue of its close proximity to a power line that has recently been built as part of the national electrification program to supply some of the important towns in the district, residents there have access to electricity.

The village has also profited from a government-initiated scheme to supply water, by means of boreholes drilled deep into the earth, to residents of the countryside. Since the water usually emanates from deep below the earth's surface it is generally considered to be clean, the only possible source of contamination being the containers in which they are collected.

Then, of course, there was the improvement in communication with the outside world brought about by the introduction of mobile phones.

On our return, the meal that Manu with the help of several willing helpers—members of our extended family as well us other residents of the little settlement—had been busy at work preparing for us was ready. It was made up of two main traditional dishes—*fufu* served with light chicken soup meant for the two adults, as well as *ampesi* (boiled plantains) and *nkontomire* (leaves from the cocoyam plant) stew for the children. She had been exceedingly generous with us—the meals served were enough to satisfy as many as ten hungry mouths!

We ate what we could and left the rest for the several children who had in the meantime gathered in the open compound to bid the visitors from Aburokyire *AKWAABA*.

We left the village just before nightfall to return to our hotel. Just as in the case of the previous day, we returned to the village around midday the next day. This time we did not encounter any problem relating to our vehicle.

Our second visit was just as exciting as the first. That was particularly so for Jonathan, who, since our move to the British Isles, seems to have been infected with the obsession of the English people for the game of football.

Not long after our arrival, as we were engaged in lively exchanges with the residents of the village who had, as on the previous day, turned up in their numbers to greet us, we heard the loud noise of drumming and singing on the street. Soon the noise grew louder and louder.

'What is going on?' I asked one of those around.

'It is the football team from Maamanso: they have just arrived for a friendly match.'

'Mpintimpi versus Maamanso? You can't be serious!'

'Yes, that is the case.'

'How dare Mpintimpi stand up to Maamanso, an encounter equivalent to David versus Goliath!'

'Doc, you will be surprised! We are going to teach them a lesson in the game of football!' Kofi Ampomah, who happened to be sitting not far from me, came in.

'Kofi, how dare your little Mpintimpi stand up to Mamaanso!'

'You just wait and see. We have a very good team here.'

Soon the procession, made up of about thirty young men, came into view, marching, dancing and making merry to the sound of cheerful music.

The team from the comparatively large town about thirty kilometres to the south-west of the little village seemed, at least judging from the optimism they were radiating, poised to thrash that of the tiny village.

On hearing what was about to happen, Jonathan began to jump around with joy. Soon he approached me.

'Do we have to pay to watch it?'

Even before I could respond to his query, Kofi, who had heard it, replied with an emphatic no!

'That is great! When will they start?'

Kofi took a look at his watch and replied, 'In about an hour.'

Fortunately he did not have to walk a great distance to watch it. As I learnt form Kofi, a new playground had been developed in an area not far from where we were.

Kofi was right in his prediction, for in the end little Mpintimpi defeated the visitors by three goals to one. (As we learnt on our second visit, the return match two weeks later ended 3–0 in favour of Mamaaso. The team from the little village seemed not to be gallant in defeat, attributing it to biased officiating!)

Notwithstanding the improvements in the economy and also in the living conditions of many in the country, Ghana remains a developing country in which poverty, particularly in the countryside, is widespread. As in the case of Mpintimpi, many in the countryside are subsistence farmers who live from hand to mouth. The main source of income in the case of residents of Mpintimpi is from the yields they obtain mostly once a year from their cocoa farms. For most of them, such earnings could be described as a drop in the huge ocean. The elderly among them, Father included, who, due to their age are no longer able to earn their own living, have to fall back on the extended family for their livelihood.

There is at the moment no pension scheme for the peasant farmers. Father, for example, spent most of his life producing cocoa beans, which were then, and still is, one of the main foreign exchange earners for the country, only to be left in his old age with practically no support from the state. He who has no children or well-to-do extended family members to fall back on is completely lost in the system. During their normal day-to-day life, these deprived members of our race go about carrying their various burdens—being it financial, material or by way of health.

The moment, however, they sense an opportunity knocking on their doors, in this case by way of the visit of someone everyone in the village regards as being enormously wealthy, they readily seize upon it. That is not to imply that the problems are feigned, as some of the problems brought to my attention illustrates.

Shortly after our arrival, one member of the extended family after the other began to make his/her request known to me. In the end, I decided to hold what I christened myself as *Social Consulting Hours* to deal with their problems. For the sake of space I will mention only a selection of the problems brought to my attention.

In the case of Father, it was a matter of money, money, money! In the meantime he had to cater for at least a dozen heads that had moved to stay with him in the spacious house he occupied.

The son of my half sister Yaa would soon be enlisted in the police service. She needed about three million cedis to acquire some of the items he needed initially and also to 'grease the palms' of some people who had been influential in his selection.

The toilet pit for use by Father and other extended family members was filled up. A new one needed to be constructed at a cost of about two million cedis.

Then there was Papito who I grew up with—indeed, my closest associate in the village. He was engaged in farming, growing oranges. His farm was small, the yields insufficient to help cater for himself, his wife and their two children. He approached me to help him establish a poultry farm. He had already done his homework. He would need an initial capital of about five million cedis approximately—500 dollars for the structure to house them as well as the initial number of young birds. I recognised a moral responsibility to help and gave him one million cedis to begin the construction. I promised to give him the rest on our scheduled visit two weeks later, depending on the progress.

There was one person who needed my urgent attention but who was not in a position to attend the consultation himself. Yes, I needed at any rate to call on Papa Kwaku, one of Father's brothers.

News had already reached me to the effect that following a massive stroke he was paralysed in both legs and arms (quadriplegic). The scene that confronted me nearly caused me, a person who by virtue of my profession has learnt to develop an emotional distance to suffering, to burst out in tears.

He lay flat on his back on a mat spread out on the floor of his room. Apart from his head, which he was still able to turn, he was incapable of any other movement. Elsewhere he would be using a special bed fit for his condition—not so under the conditions I have on several occasions made mention of in this book.

Elsewhere, he would be cared for by specially trained personnel paid for by the state; not so in his situation.

There was one thing he could still count on, however—the solidarity of his family, both nuclear and extended. Indeed, one of his daughters had given up her work and had returned to the village to assume round the clock care. She was being assisted by her mother and several other members of the extended family.

One thing I noticed, though—Uncle, who before the stroke was a head teacher of an elementary school in a town not far away, was still mentally very active and could engage me in lively conversation, recalling a short period in my educational career when I stayed with him in Afosu to enable me to attend the elementary school there.

How I wished I could take him along with me to Europe so he could have access to more appropriate care. For the moment, though, I could only do what was in my position to do, namely to contribute a few hundred thousand cedis towards his care.

It was during the consulting hours at Mpintimpi that Karen, who naturally was not familiar with the concept of sharing in the African context, came up with the term *financial suicide*. Yes, as she watched me part with one substantial sum after the other to help solve the problems of one extended family member after the other, she looked at me and said: 'Papa, you are doing nothing other than committing *financial suicide!*'

She was not far from right! So long as I had an escape route, namely the ability to escape from the fire and return to Europe to regenerate my finances, I could allow the knot to pull on my neck, certain that at the very last minute I could free myself.

What, however, would be the situation when I finally returned to settle there, in the very midst of the storm with no rescue boats around?

For the moment, however, we could end our visit to the troubled zone and head back to our hotel at Nkawkaw, notwithstanding the fact that our consultation had depleted our coffers of a good five million cedis (about five hundred dollars)!

CHAPTER 21
The Good Guess of a Trusted Friend

W e left Nkawkaw in the morning of 30th July to travel to Mim, to Rita's hometown. The plan was to first make a short stopover at a little town on the northern outskirts of Kumasi. We wanted to call on Kwasi at his place of work and secondly use his Internet connection to carry out a very important transaction in the UK. The journey to Kumasi, about one hundred kilometres away, was uneventful.

Kumasi, the second largest city in the country, capital of the Ashantis, had experienced a significant facelift since our last visit in 1994. Like Accra, the road network had undergone a considerable improvement. The roads were also congested with traffic; several new buildings as well as those under construction could be seen everywhere. The degree of transformation did not match the phenomenal change Accra had undergone, however.

It was a great delight to meet Kwasi again. We first came in contact in July 1988 when I was a student at Hannover Medical School in Germany. He had just finished his medical studies in the then Soviet Union and had come to the teaching hospital of the northern German city for a short stay aimed at gaining further experience in his field. He returned to Ghana shortly after our meeting to take up an appointment as a junior doctor.

The last time we saw each other was in 1991. At that time he was working as a junior doctor at the newly opened Cardiac Thoracic Unit of the Korle Bu Teaching Hospital. I was in Ghana to do an elective at Ghana's leading hospital and took up residence in the grounds of the hospital. Kwasi and Georgina, his wife, who also lived in a Junior Doctors' residency not far from where I resided, were a great help to me. Not long after that meeting Kwasi was transferred to the Ashanti Region.

He welcomed us heartily into his residence. He occupied a large bungalow boasting two large bedrooms, a study, a large living room, a kitchen, shower and toilet. As if that were not enough, he had an additional building, a boys' quarters attached to it! That indeed was spacious accommodation!

'It is the residence of the District Medical Officer!' Kwasi pointed out.

'That indeed befits his status!' I remarked.

'I rarely sleep here, though. At the moment we provide only outpatient care. As you have realised, this place is only a stone's throw from Kumasi. Georgina, who works in the accounts department of the Kwame Nkrumah University of Science and Technology, has a bungalow about the size of this one assigned to her. It is only on rare occasions when I need to do something urgently before the next day, that I stay here overnight to get it done.' He smiled, seeing my surprise, and continued: 'Things may change in the foreseeable future, however. You probably saw the nicely painted building block a few metres from this one. It is our new labour and minor surgery unit. Almost everything needed to run it is now in place. When things get going I may have to stay overnight from time to time.'

I could not hide my admiration of the progress he had made since our last meeting.

'You are doing quite well, friend!' I made my feelings known.

'Well, things have not always been easy. Matters were particularly rough during the first several months after our return form Europe. Apart from having to adjust to the new working climate, we had to fight hard to make ends meet. Fortunately, we returned with two vehicles I managed to purchase from the money I earned doing some odd jobs in London. We decided to use one as a Taxi. The extra earnings from it helped us keep above water.

'What was true then is true today—one can hardly survive on one's salary here. Although my salary has risen considerably over the years, the corresponding rise in the cost of living has neutralized the gains.'

'Somehow I do envy your position,' I said. 'You are at home within your own people; you are not just an ordinary citizen but a highly regarded one for that matter; besides that, you are privileged to enjoy the warm and stable weather here. Finally I have also noticed a significant improvement in the standard of living here. Indeed, with enough means at one's disposal, I think one can live quite a comfortable life here.'

'Yes, indeed, things have improved considerably over the last several years. As you are aware, in former times money chased the few items around. Now, in today's Ghana, one can purchase almost anything provided one has the means.'

'I have realised, though, that the prices demanded for some of the items on sale here compare favourably with those being demanded in Europe for similar items. This is true even for foodstuffs; in some cases I have even discovered that certain food items are even more expensive here than in Europe. For example, the other day we bought a whole fried chicken for 60000 cedis: that amounts to about six dollars. Now, according to my information, the official minimum wage is 19000 cedis or approximately two dollars. That means that one has to work three whole days to be able to purchase a fried chicken! Chicken which should be regarded as a basic food item has thus become a luxury!'

'That is exactly the situation; the goods abound on the market but for the ordinary persons they are just like items displayed at a museum— they are out of his reach. The country is developing into a parallel society where the rich and the poor have no point of intersection.'

'But food should be cheap! We have enough fertile land to produce abundant food at prices affordable to everyone.'

'The very little food produced here is exported to Europe. I am indeed in favour of free trade. In my opinion, however, the government needs to regulate the market to make sure there is first enough cheap food around before it is exported. Those Ghanaians who have left to settle in Europe should either become accustomed to the meals produced there or should come back home to assist in national development rather than parasite on the little food we produce here.'

Next, I turned the discussion to an area relevant to both of us, namely the health sector. I had read about the introduction of a health insurance scheme into the country. I wanted to find out more about it from the expert on the 'battlefront.'

'I read about the introduction of the Health Insurance scheme in the county,' I began. 'How does it work?'

'Indeed the scheme was launched personally by the president in March 2004. An adult has to pay a monthly minimum subscription to be covered. The rate is currently 75000 cedis. Children of parents who both subscribe to the scheme are also covered.'

'How is that accepted by the populace?'

'It is a mixed picture. Some think they are either too young or healthy or both to fall sick so decide to save their money rather than join. There are others who subscribe initially, but are not able to keep up the monthly payments. There are still those who, though willing to subscribe, lack the means to do so.'

'Doesn't the state come in such situations to offer a helping hand?'

'Yes, it does. But not everyone fulfils the state criteria for assistance. It covers the very aged as well as those who fulfil certain other conditions. Those who are poor but are unable to comply with the government's criteria for assistance are left out.'

'Still, I think it's a step in the right direction.'

'Indeed it is—in particular, when one compares it to the *cash and carry* period. At that time one could either afford to pay for medical treatment or one was left to die.

'This scheme has brought about an unexpected side effect, however. Many a person, once they have paid their contributions, think they have the right to medical care, even when they cannot be considered to be sick.

'I have witnessed several instances when a father, mother and all their children have all turned up in my consulting hours claiming they are all unwell. When I take their medical history and carry out the examination, I get the impression some of them, if not all of them, are just pretending. Either they are there with the intention of collecting medication for their uninsured relatives, or just to acquire the medication to be hoarded at home.'

'That can't be true!!'

'Well, that unfortunately is the case. It has led to a rapid increase in the number of patients seeking medical help these days. Prior to the introduction of the scheme patients used to hide their diseases for lack of money; now they turn up for treatment at the slightest sign of disease.'

Just as we were engaged in this lively exchange, there was a knock on the door. A young man aged about twenty entered. In his hands was a plastic bag. He placed it on a large dining table in one corner of the living room.

'That is yours. You enjoy it. I will hurry back to my office to get one or two things done. Give me a call when you are through.'

Without our knowledge he had ordered some meals for us, bless him. And as if he knew what the children liked most, he had ordered the very meals that ranked high among their favourites—jolof rice and fried chicken. It was very much enjoyed by all, for it wasn't any ordinary jolof rice meal, but one prepared by one who, judging by the taste of the meal we were privileged to enjoy, should be counted among the most seasoned cooks!

After the meal, I used Kwasi's Internet facilities to carry out an important transaction. In the process I visited the site www.ghanaweb. com where I learned that the Ghanaian authorities and Lufthansa had, a few days earlier, amicably resolved their differences. Lufthansa had in the meantime resumed its flights into the country. As far as we were concerned, however, it was news of no relevance, at least not during that particular stay in Ghana.

Finally, at about 1500 hrs, we begged permission to leave.

'I thought you wanted to spend the night here?' Kwasi said. 'Indeed, everything is set for you. You have two big bedrooms at your disposal.'

'We shall definitely return to spend a night or two with you. I have not seen Georgina and the children yet. Rita and the children also need to get to know them. For today, however, we want to move on—especially for Rita's sake. After spending almost two weeks in the country she can hardly wait to meet her people.'

CHAPTER 22
A Lone Irishman's Adventure to the Gold Coast

꿏

S oon we parted company with Kwasi and headed back to Kumasi to join the road that would take us to our final destination – Mim. Boasting a population of a little over 22000 residents based on the 2000 census, it is one of the urban centres of the Brong Ahafo region. It is located about 130 kilometres to the northwest of Kumasi.

As we drove away from Kumasi the picture of a deserted country became even more evident. On our previous visit thirteen years before we travelled about the same time on the same road. The road was quite busy. Not so on this occasion: traffic on the main road leading to Sunyani, the capital of the Brong Ahafo region, was unexpectedly sparse.

I was even more impressed by the green vegetation that stretched over several kilometres on each side of the road. The thick canopy was interrupted in several places by large trees displaying straight, smooth trunks, some of which reached several metres above the earth's surface.

With such fertile land at our disposal, what was preventing us from putting up huge palm, orange, cocoa plantations instead of leaving the land to lie barren and uncultivated? Couldn't we place capital and needed machinery in the hands of able-bodied young men and women hawking on the streets of Accra to till the land instead of running up and down the streets of Accra?

It was a little after 19:00 hrs when we pulled up at Mim. Rita's extended family occupies a prominent position in her hometown. They happen to have the right to the Stool of the Omanhene or Paramount chief of the Mim traditional area.

In Ghana communities are headed by traditional leaders. In a small village or town the leader is called a chief or odikro. The Omanhene of an area exercises authority over several other chiefs and subchiefs of the traditional area

The traditional ruler is the embodiment of the values, norms and ethics of the community and represents their aspirations, anxieties and ambitions. He resolves personal, social and to some extent the economic problems of his subjects. Traditional leaders—chiefs, kings, queens—usually enjoy the absolute loyalty of their subjects. Even though democratic institutions such as local councils as well as district and regional assemblies now represent the state on the local, district and regional levels, even to this day the traditional ruler continues to command considerable authority and respect. Indeed, as far as those they rule over are concerned, they still combine executive, legislative and judicial powers. Traditional rulers are neither elected by their subjects nor appointed by the state. The position is rather passed over by way of inheritance. In Ghana, depending on the ethnic group involved, the position could be inherited patrilineally or matrilineally.

The Akans, the main ethnic group in south and central Ghana, pass their inheritance along the line of the female. Since in their case inheritance is by way of the line of the female members of the traditional family, theoretically Rita could one day be crowned queen of the area. In the same vein, David or Jonathan could one day become Omanhene or Paramount chief of the area; Karen, on her part, could occupy the Stool of Queen of the area.

The original plan was to first call on Rita's extended family home before continuing on to our accommodation. Due to a sudden downpour of torrential rains as we approached the town, however, we decided to head straight for our accommodation and postpone the family reunion until the next morning.

Arrangements concerning our accommodation had been made prior to our arrival in the country. Although there was enough space in the extended family home to accommodate us, for the sake of convenience we chose to occupy one of the bungalows on the estates of the main business enterprise in the town Ayum Timbers, which boasted a wood-processing factory on the outskirts of the town.

Still well known by many through its previous name Mim Timbers, it was established by an Irishman named Desmond Charmant, who settled in the Gold Coast years before it gained its independence. He had acquired a huge area of virgin tropical forest from the traditional leader of the town. To process the abundant tropical wood on his property, he established Mim Timbers in 1947.

He did not restrict his activities to the processing of wood alone but soon became involved in the cultivation of the land as well as the rearing of animals. Soon he would become an important supplier of foodstuffs such as plantains, yams, cassava as well as oranges and palm products, not only locally, but also on the wider Ghanaian market. He was also successful in animal husbandry and was soon producing eggs, poultry, sheep and cattle in commercial quantities. He no doubt had the welfare of his workers at heart, putting up several bungalows on his huge estates to accommodate many of them.

In due course his business flourished to the point of gaining national attention. Did he become a victim of his own success? Whatever the case may be, the fact is that in 1978 the then ruling military government of Gen Acheampong nationalised the Mim Timbers.

Desmond, as he was popularly known, continued with his farming enterprise, still producing all kinds of plant and animal products for the market. With the fortunes of the state-owned Mim Timber falling partly as a result of mismanagement, the government, then embarking on a large-scale privatisation process in 1996, sold the company to a private investor who renamed it Ayum Timbers. Although Mr Desmond Charmant has in the meantime passed away, the name Desmond is still a household word in the town. It was one of the bungalows on the estates of the timber-processing factory that we were booked into at a fee of approximately ten dollars per night.

The semi-detached building boasted a large living room and two equally large bedrooms. Although the building was built several years ago, the sewage and bathroom facilities were still in good order. Indeed, it was only in that lodging that we enjoyed an optimal supply of hot water throughout our stay.

As I learnt form Rita, even before the introduction of electricity to the town, the residents of the estates of the enterprise had access to electricity, being connected to the huge generator that supplied power to the machines of the factory. It goes without saying therefore that we were privileged to have enjoyed an uninterrupted electricity supply throughout our stay, unlike residents of the town who depended entirely on power from the national grid and, like everyone else in the country, were subjected to the frequent power cuts in line with the then ongoing nationwide rationalisation of power.

CHAPTER 23
The Young Man with the
European Visa Application Forms

🙣

The next day we made our way to the main traditional home of Rita's extended family. By virtue of it being the residence of the Paramount Chief, it is also the palace or *ahenfie*. The chiefs and sub chiefs of the area, forming the Mim Traditiona Council, call on the Omanhene regularly to discuss matters pertaining to the welfare of the general community.

As might be expected, we were warmly welcomed by Rita's people. She also boasts a large extended family. Her maternal grandmother, of whom she has fond memories, gave birth to several children. They in turn produced several children. Though they have become 'globalised'— some are resident in the US, UK, Germany, among other countries—a considerable number of them still reside in the Ahenfie. After her long period of absence she, too, needed someone to help her make out to whom the several children who greeted us belonged.

I shall not try the readers' patience with a detailed account of all that we experienced in Rita's hometown. A great deal of that was almost a repetition of what we went through at Mpintimpi. Just as was the case in Mpintmipi, we had to go on a ritual walkabout through the town shaking one hand after the other! Due to the comparatively larger size of Mim we had to be selective as to who we visited—restricting ourselves to Rita's relations as well as friends and associates of old.

In regard to Jonathan, there was also no change of behaviour—as at Mpintimpi, he went about chasing cats, goats, sheep, fowls and all other domesticated animals that came his way. The reader may want to know whether we also had to hold a 'consulting hour'! Yes indeed! In this case, however, for the sake of fairness, I played only a passive role and left Rita herself to sort out matters with her own people. In the end our social plan reduced our purchasing power by just about the same sum as it did in my village.

Still, I consider a couple of issues that cropped up in our interaction with her family worthy of highlighting. On the second day of our visit to the extended family home, we were greeted by a young man in his early twenties. Surprised to see him, Rita began:

'I have been told that you are now resident in Accra.'

'Yes auntie!' he replied, smiling.

'What are you doing here then?'

'Well, I learnt that you came to look for us in Accra. At that time I was not at home. I was expecting you to call again, but unfortunately you didn't. Two days ago, word reached me that you were heading here, so I decided to chase you here!'

'But that was not necessary! After all, we shall spend some time in Accra before returning finally to Europe.'

'Well, I have an issue that demands immediate attention so I decided to meet you without delay.'

'What is the problem?'

'Well, the chance has come for me to travel to Europe. Unfortunately the means at my disposal is not sufficient. I have therefore decided to contact you for financial assistance.'

'Which part of Europe?'

'Spain.'

'Have you obtained a visa?'

'Not yet. The plan is to travel to either the Czech Republic or Switzerland. From there I will attempt to move on to my final destination.'

'Have you obtained a Czech or Swiss visa?'

'Plans have reached an advanced stage.'

'Do you have any supporting documents?'

'Yes indeed.'

'Okay, you can bring them to our residence tomorrow for us to examine them.'

He turned up as arranged the next day. He handed us a large DIN 4 envelope he was carrying. Enclosed in it were two unfilled visa application forms—one for Switzerland, the other for the Czech Republic!

'But I thought you said your plans to obtain those visas were already advanced!'

'I only need the money: I have all the documents that will guarantee me the visa!'

'Well, assuming you make it to either country, what is the chance of proceeding to Spain?'

'I hope to find my way there!'

'How?'

'Time will tell!'

'I am afraid you seem to be living in a fool's paradise!'

'Believe me, I will make it.'

Both of us could only gaze at him in astonishment for his blatant refusal to face reality.

Rita decided to turn to another issue—that of money.

'How much money is involved?'

'Five million cedis.'

'And how much have you raised yourself?'

'About a million!'

'So you expect me to help out with the rest?' She shook her head. 'I am afraid I am not in a position to help. Even should I be in a position to do so, I would prefer to invest my resources in ventures that have a good chance of success.'

He was definitely not convinced by our answer, for a few days after the meeting his mother approached her cousin to re-present his plea.

'Your nephew is very disappointed that you could not help him realise his plans of travelling to Aburokyire to seek greener pastures," she said. "He says he stands a very good chance of succeeding should he overcome the present financial hurdle.'

'Have you convinced yourself about his claims?'

'Well, he showed me some papers to prove his case.'

'Did you read them?'

'No; still, I have no cause to believe that he is not telling the truth.'

'Well, I live in Europe so I am aware of the conditions prevailing there. Your son can show nothing apart from visa forms. That is nothing at all; indeed, you yourself can travel to the Czech or Swiss embassy in Accra tomorrow and ask for them.' Judging from the look on her face, she still seemed unconvinced.

CHAPTER 24
Absentee Farmer

W
as it because I was mesmerized by the abundant green vegetation that confronted us wherever we drove? Was it because of the abundant fertile land? Or was it because, somehow, I wanted to contribute my little quota to help bring down the price of food that I still considered too high in comparison with the earnings of the average worker? Food indeed was not a scarce commodity in the country. My impression, though, was that the price at which food items were sold had no bearing on the prevailing official minimum wage.

Whatever the reason, I gradually developed an interest in farming during the course of my stay. With the necessary capital input, one could for example go into commercial cattle farming, since grass and fields to feed the cattle on abounds. The same applies to poultry, sheep rearing, etc.

As I mentioned earlier, the land is suitable for the growth of several types of tropical crops—banana, plantains, cocoa, mangoes, oranges, palm—in large quantities. The problem of the subsistence farmer in Ghana, however, is that of capital input. I remember as I was growing up in Mpintimpi we always relied on the rain to water our crops. If Father could afford a simple water-pumping machine we might have been independent of the rains and have produced higher yields of our crops. The same was true for clearing the forest, to get it ready for cultivation. Father, for example, had to rely on manpower and a small axe to fell the large trees growing on the land to prepare it for cultivation.

I made my intention known to Inspector, Rita's uncle on her mother's side. 'What use is the land, farmland, in the Ahafo area?' he said. 'It is not for nothing that many refer to the Brong Ahafo region as the breadbasket of the country. Fertile land abounds here, yes. The problem is money and those willing to engage in farming. We are getting older and older. The young have deserted us for Accra and elsewhere. In former times food was abundant on our local market. That is no longer the case these days.'

'You keep your ears open for some one selling his or her land,' I said.

'You get your money ready!' he replied.

Inspector was soon proved right. A few days after our conversation we called on him again. Shortly after we had taken a seat, Inspector called me to his living room.

'I was approached yesterday by a young man keen on selling his farmland,' he announced. 'On hearing about our visitors from Aburokyire, he approached me to ask me to inquire from you whether you might be interested in purchasing it.' 'Yes indeed—provided of course we can agree on a price affordable to us,' I stated.

In the end we agreed to inspect the land in question the following morning.

The next day, accompanied by a handful of Rita's relations as well as the owner and his uncle, we set out to inspect the property. We travelled in the *tro tro*. After driving about twenty kilometres along a newly constructed tarred road I was told to turn left and follow a road, the condition of which contrasted greatly with the one we were leaving. Not only was it untarred, it was narrow, uneven and had potholes in several places.

Furious as a result of the poor state of the road, one of the passengers began to vent his anger at the member of parliament of the area.

'These politicians care little about us, the rural population! They seem to have forgotten that our economy relies to some extent on the cocoa and other cash crops we produce here.'

'Put your complaint in writing; extend an invitation to him to come round to see things for himself.'

'He won't mind you! At least not at a time when an election is not pending.'

'And,' another in the group remarked, 'even when he turns up for an election campaign he wont feel the full effect of the poor road, for he will be travelling in a 4x4.'

After following the road, which passed through a predominantly thick tropical forest over a distance of about eight kilometres, I was asked to turn left in about a hundred metres.

'But there is no sign of a road on the left side!' I said to the person who had instructed me to do so.

'Yes there is! You may call it a bush path, but it is broad enough to allow vehicular traffic. Indeed, from time to time vehicles travel on it to the village it is leading to.'

'Probably jeeps, landrovers and other 4X4's, but not a Mercedes mini-bus!'

'Don't be scared, Doc! We shall make it.'

'Well, you have to push it, should it get stuck!'

The road indeed was broad enough to permit us to drive along it; the bush in the middle of it was quite tall, however, and in some places scraped on the underside of the vehicle.

After manoeuvring my way along the rough and rugged terrain over a distance of about three kilometres, I breathed a sigh of relief as I sighted a handful of buildings in the distance.

'Thank God we have made it!' someone at the back cried with joy.

The little settlement was about the size of two football pitches. It boasted about ten brick houses.

We were greeted warmly by the dwellers, who obviously were delighted by the rare visit of a vehicle to their settlement.

As I discovered in the course of our stay, a good cross section of the population of Ghana was represented there. For example, there was the owner of the property we were about to inspect, a member of the Twi-speaking Akans who form the majority ethnic group in the country, a handful of Gas who make up the original population of the Greater Accra region, as well as a pair who had travelled from the Dagomba area of northern Ghana to become caretakers for some of the cocoa farms in the area.

We were greeted warmly by my business partner who was introduced by his first name, Yaw. I was surprised by his relatively young age.

Indeed, I put his age at approximately thirty-five years. I wondered how a person of his age could have cultivated cocoa that had already reached maturity. From my own experience working on Father's cocoa farm I knew the species of cocoa under consideration requires several years to reach maturity. I was keen to find out more about his background.

It was not the time for probing questions, however.

'Come on, let's get to business,' Inspector, the eldest member of the group, began. 'Take us straight to inspect the land.'

We followed the property owner along a bush path leading from the village. After following for about a hundred metres, the property owner said: 'We are there. Get ready while I show you round it.' In all it took us about an hour to inspect the whole property, made up in the main of secondary forest.

I wondered what was to follow next. Without any plan in hand, I was completely at a loss as to the appropriate price to offer. I confided my thoughts to one of the leading figures in my 'negotiating team'.

'Don't worry, Doc, I have in the past helped others buy farmland. I have an idea how much it should cost. Anything above that should be rejected out of hand.'

I decided to leave my negotiating team, made up of Inspector and Rita's brother-in-law, to do the bargaining. After about twenty minutes of hard bargaining the transaction was finally sealed. Payment would be by means of instalments made over several months.

Just as we were celebrating the cut deal, Yaw turned to me and said: 'Since I have decided to turn my back on farming forever, I want to dispose of all my farmland. I have another piece of land nearby. It is smaller than the one I have just sold. Would you be interested in it?'

Even before I could reply someone in the group expressed his displeasure: 'Not today, friend—another time! I am exhausted, I just want to get back home.' In the end we agreed to return in three days to inspect it.

I was curious to know something about Yaw's background and in particular how he came to own the piece of land so I called him aside from the group. 'You are quite a young man,' I began. 'How then did you manage to own this piece of land?'

'I inherited it from my late grandfather; he passed it on in his will.'

'He must have been very fond of you! You were not his only grandchild, were you?'

'You are right; there were several of us. He also had his own children to consider—and he had several children. Somehow, however, he decided to bestow his property on me and a selected few of his children.'

'You must have been very close to his heart! Tell me, what did you possess that the others did not?'

'If I am permitted to mention them: they are patience, tolerance and humility.' He smiled and continued, 'Grandfather was generally regarded by all who knew him as being very demanding and difficult to deal with. It turned out that I was among the few persons who could deal with him. I was forbearing in my dealings with him, not allowing myself to be provoked by his frequent outbursts of temper. As it turned out my equanimity and tolerance paid off. When, towards the end of his life he made his plans known to the rest of the family, many could not believe their ears. He was adamant, though. "He is going to get what I have assigned him and no one else!" he declared to the astonishment and envy of some members of the extended family.'

'Why then do you want to part with it?'

'Indeed, I did not reach this conclusion lightly and only after months of serious wrestling with myself. In the end, however, I decided that I would be better off disposing of it and using the proceeds from it to start a different life. The reality is that the land has turned out to be too big for me.'

'What do you mean by that?'

'Well, in order to be able to utilise such a large piece of land effectively, considerable capital input, mainly in the form of cash, is required. That is particularly important to pay for the additional hands needed to work on it. Unfortunately this has not been forthcoming.'

'Why didn't you contact the banks?'

'The banks! My understanding is that they give credit to only those who have accounts with them.'

'You could have opened one!'

'It is easier said than done! They require those wishing to do so to deposit an initial minimum amount. I have not been able to raise it. The

137

result is that though I inherited the property almost twenty years ago, I have not been able make any meaningful use of it.'

'What are your immediate plans? You must be very careful with the money you are about to get. As the saying goes, money has a way of taking wings and flying!'

'My plan is to move to Kumasi, acquire a *tro-tro* and go into the transport business!'

'Can you drive on your own?'

'No.'

'Be warned, my friend, in regard to the driver you entrust your vehicle to. Everyone I have spoken to has advised me to be weary of the *tro-tro* drivers. As they put it, a good proportion of them will just *"drive the vehicle into their pockets!"*

'Well, initially, I will entrust it to my nephew. In the meantime I will learn how to drive myself: after about six months I will take over myself.'

'Well, friend, I really do wish you well. I do not want to buy your land today only to find you tomorrow by the wayside begging for money. As a way of helping you manage your money well, I will arrange with you to go to a bank and help you open an account. I won't hand a pesewa[4] of the agreed amount as cash into your hands. Rather I will transfer it by way of instalments, based on an agreed formula.'

'That is very nice of you.'

'I will advise you to spend part of the proceeds to acquire the vehicle, and keep the rest in the bank. Make a firm resolve not to touch the money in the bank over a fixed period of time no matter what. It requires a lot of self-discipline to achieve that, but it is essential for your future.'

Just then I noticed him turn his attention towards the *tro tro* parked not far from where we were. He looked at it for a while. Then he turned to me.

'I have a suggestion,' he said.

'Okay, go ahead.'

---

[4]   100 pesewas = 1 Cedi

'Why not exchange your bus as part payment for the farm? It is exactly this type of vehicle I am planning to use in my *tro-tro* business. You will then need to pay the remaining amount into my account.'

His proposal was so unexpected that for a moment I was at a loss as to what to say. In the end I asked him to give me time, till our next meeting, to consider it. As we drove back to Mim I thought over his idea. On the surface, it was a fair deal. I had my strong reservations, however. I was not unaware of the mentality of my people. So long as everything went well with the vehicle, no one was expected to murmur. Not so, should things begin to go bad with the vehicle. After all, it was a second-hand vehicle. Besides that not all the roads in the country could be classified with the best. That may well lead to mechanical problems— affecting the engine, the gears, the exhaust pipe, the electrical connections, the shock absorber—one could go on listing them. The moment those problems begin to crop up, he would be sure to go round casting insinuations on our name—'They are cheats, he and his wife! They deliberately exchanged a vehicle they knew was worn out for my precious farmland! Cold-hearted swindlers they are!'

No, I thought, his proposal was unacceptable! I would stretch my resources to pay him in cash. He could then use the proceeds to look out for a vehicle of his choice. As far as finding the type of vehicle we were using, he had no need to worry. He only needed to travel to Kumasi or Accra to find several of them lined up on the streets, desperately looking for buyers! Rita completely concurred with my way of thinking.

'No way!' she began. 'We shall keep our vehicle. What is the guarantee that a thirteen-year-old vehicle will meet his high expectations? It is a matter involving his livelihood. Very soon my name will be on the lips of everyone on the streets of Mim. "How could such well-to-do's take advantage of a poor disadvantaged peasant in such an unkind manner?" he and everyone else could go about accusing us.'

We set out early in the morning of the third day as planned for the little village. This time the journey would not be without incident. A heavy downpour the previous day rendered the untarred road muddy and slippery in several places. Pools of water had also collected in the countless potholes. Still, we managed to make progress until we were about five kilometres from our destination.

The first problem cropped up as we tried to ascend a steep drive. The surface of the road at that point was not only rugged, but muddy. I changed to bottom gear and pressed on the accelerator. Initially it looked as if we would make it. My optimism turned out to be premature.

Midway between the bottom and the apex of the rise, the rear wheels got stuck in mud. Try as I might, the vehicle would not move. Moments later we spotted a fully packed mini-bus approaching from the opposite direction.

Initially, I thought the driver would stop and get out to inspect the road before advancing. No, he moved on and my heart missed a beat! How on earth would he manage to drive the fully packed mini-bus down the steep slippery slope? Well, the driver would soon prove me wrong and demonstrate in practical terms why he and the few other drivers plying that road have managed to remain in business despite the rough terrain they operate on.

Slowly, slowly, he progressed down the slope, skilfully avoiding one slippery patch as well as one pothole after the other. Hurray! He managed finally to steer his vehicle to safety.

I thought he would drive on leaving us to our fate. No! Solidarity with one another seemed to be the motto of the drivers operating under the prevailing harsh conditions. As soon as he had put the slope behind him, he pulled his vehicle to a stop. He got out and hurried to our aid. Almost all the able-bodied passengers followed suit.

First, the driver approached me to give me some tips as to the best driving style that I should adopt. Then he gave the order for the approximately twenty hands to go into action.

'One, two, three, push!' he ordered

Try as they might, the vehicle would not move.

After a while the driver returned to me.

'Sir, I suggest you hand over the control of the vehicle to me and that I take over the steering from you; we know the conditions on this road and are thus better acquainted with driving on it.'

'I have nothing against that,' I replied and jumped out of the vehicle to join hands with the rest.

With about a dozen pair of hands forcefully at work and a driver experienced with how to overcome the challenges of the rugged road behind the wheels, the horsepower of the powerful diesel engine combined with concerted human power, proved too powerful a match for the slippery mud. Soon the vehicle was freed from the mud.

So once again we were on our way. That would not be the end of the matter for that day, however! The downpour had taken its toll on the state of the three-kilometre stretch of bush path as well. On two occasions, to and from the farm, we got stuck and had to give the vehicle a push.

The other piece of land for sale was comparatively smaller than the previous one. It was planted with maize ready for harvesting in a few weeks' time. According to Yaw, someone from a neighbouring village had approached him several months before, asking him to lend it out to him to enable him to cultivate the crops. The agreement was to share the produce equally amongst landowner and cultivator.

This time it did not take us long to agree on the price. Contrary to the previous day, Yaw this time demanded immediate payment. He needed the money to settle a debt, the repayment of which was long overdue.

With the sale of his land, Yaw was free to put life in the remote jungle behind him and follow several thousand others into the city in the hope of achieving an improved lifestyle and prospects. In comparison with the great majority of others, however, he was setting out under much more favourable circumstances. With proper planning, hard work, self-discipline and some degree of luck, he had a significant advantage over the others.

He was disappointed, though, to learn that I had not agreed to his deal and that I was going to keep the vehicle. I was sticking to my principles. Still, I was keen to make sure he made good use of his money. On my insistence, he opened an account with one of the local banks. Several weeks have elapsed since then and my information is that he is moving very cautiously towards the realisation of his goal.

I thought those would be the only two parcels of land I would acquire during my stay. Well, as it turned out, that thought was premature.

CHAPTER 25
Terms Redefined

Two days prior to our final departure, we visited Rita's extended family home as usual. As it turned dark, we were planning to leave for our accommodation, when Inspector approached me.

'Someone wants to speak to you. She wants some confidentiality, so she is waiting in my room.'

I followed him there. Seated on one of his sofas was a lady whose age I put at about fifty. After we were seated, Inspector turned to her and said, 'Though you have revealed to me the reason for your coming, still tradition demands that you tell us why you are here.'

'I have come to solicit the help of our respected visitor in a difficulty situation. I need as a matter of urgency 10 million cedis. I need the money to enable my son to embark on a journey to Aburokyire. All the necessary arrangements concerning his trip—the passport, the ticket, the visa, etc.—are complete. What we need now is sufficient hard currency that he can show at the immigration on his arrival. So far I have financed the undertaking with my own means and also money I borrowed from my acquaintances. The loans attract high interests though; in some instances, I am required to re-pay double the amount lent out.

Just as I was considering taking an additional loan, Yaw, my nephew, told me about the transaction between himself and Doc. After pondering over it for a while, I have decided also to sell a piece of cocoa farmland instead of taking out an additional loan. I have therefore come to find out whether Doc is interested in acquiring an additional piece of farmland.'

After she had finished talking, Inspector turned to me and remarked, 'Well, the ball is in your court, Doc.' I began to consider my response. I would ask her to give me time to talk it over with Rita, I thought. In the meantime, I would ask her to tell me briefly something about her son's intended journey.

'You're willing to sell your property to help your son travel to Aburokyire?'

'Yes, indeed.'

'Which part of Aburokyire?'

She stared at me, somewhat confused.

'I can't remember the name anymore. It's a long one. I'll bring him along next time. You will be able to hear it from the camel's own mouth.'

'What is he going to do there?'

'In search of greener pastures, of course. Our hope is that he will be able to find something meaningful in order to be in a position to assist those left behind!'

If only I could dissuade her—and her son—from their plans! I was fully aware however that at that stage in their preparation, nothing—indeed nothing—would lead them to change their minds. I even stood the danger of being branded selfish should I try to warn her concerning the difficulties that an unskilled person like her son would face should he make it to the West.

I realised that if I represented the prospects prevailing in Aburokyire as very poor, she would question our appearance of success. Why all the wealth we seemed to be displaying—a Mercedes mini-bus (never mind if it was already more than fourteen years old)? How were we able to wear quite good clothing and, to top it all, have the ability to purchase her cousin's farmland at a price the average resident in the village could hardly afford? Clearly Aburokyire had worked for us!

I decided to bargain for time, time that would enable me to talk the matter over with the rest of the family.

'Could you pleases give me some time to consider the proposal?' I said after a while.

'But I hear you are leaving tomorrow!'

'No, not tomorrow; the day after tomorrow.'

'But you need to inspect the land first; if you could make up your mind tonight, we could inspect it tomorrow. Then I will know whether to rely on you or contact someone else. The money should be ready on Monday at all costs, and today is already Friday!'

'Give me the night to think over it. If I agree in principle to purchase it, I will ask some members of Rita's extended family to accompany you to inspect the land on my behalf, possibly tomorrow or else on Sunday. I will leave the amount you urgently need with one of Rita's relations. Should they find the farm suitable to be purchased and you agree on the price, that person will hand the money over to you in good time to enable your son to embark on his journey. The rest will follow in due course.'

In the end we agreed to meet at the same place and at the same time the next day.

As we emerged from the room, Rita, who had been looking for me, flounced into us. She greeted my companion heartily, surprised to see the lady. She was no stranger to her since her home was situated not far from that of her own family.

'What does she want from you?' she inquired when we were alone

'She is offering her cocoa farm for sale!'

'That cannot be true!'

'That is exactly the case!'

'Very soon everyone will be asking us to purchase their farmland! Quite a lot of them are plagued with financial burdens. The moment word gets round that a well-to-do Burger is in town looking for farmland to buy, they will line up at our doorstep.'

'If only the banks in the UK were prepared to dish out loans.'

'Why is she offering her land for sale?'

'To enable her child to travel to Aburokyire!'

'You don't mean it!'

'Yes indeed; he is already sitting on his packed luggage.'

'Where is he heading for?'

'She couldn't tell me. She says it has slipped her memory. She will bring him along tomorrow so that I can hear it from the donkey' s own mouth.'

'Did you promise anything?'

'No. I asked her to give me tonight to talk it over with you.'

'What do you think?'

'I would like to go for it, based on the recommendation of those who go to inspect it. If we don't buy it, she will look out for other buyers. She is just desperate for money. Her son has to make it to Aburokyire at all costs.'

'Do we have enough money to do so?'

'Well, we will have to stretch our resources. It is an investment worth making, certainly.'

The next day we met at Inspector's hall as agreed. Her son was visibly absent.

'I thought you were going to bring your son along?' I asked her as soon as we were seated.

'Yes, indeed. Unfortunately about half an hour before we were to leave for here, he had to leave home to attend to something else at another end of the town. After waiting in vain for him to return, I decided to come alone. I have left word behind requesting him to proceed here on his return.'

She paused for a while. Finally she put the question I had been expecting.

'Any good news?' she inquired nervously.

'Yes indeed; we have agreed in principle to purchase your farm.'

I could read the signs of relief on her face.

'My son will be delighted to hear that! Thank you so much! I am so grateful.'

'As I made it clear yesterday, I will go ahead with the purchase only on the recommendation of the delegation which will inspect the land on my behalf. They have in the meantime agreed to do so on Sunday. They will contact you in due course regarding the time and place to meet. As I also promised during our last meeting, I will leave the sum urgently needed by you with a relative of Rita's to be handed over as the case may be.'

Just then we heard a knock on the door. Inspector bade the person at his door enter.

In stepped a tall, well-built young man aged about twenty years.

'Meet my young and adventurous young son, Doc!' his mother exclaimed.

The joy in her face was clearly visible. The newcomer greeted us politely and took a seat near his mother.

'Young man, your mother tells me you are on your way out of the country?'

'Yes indeed,' he replied in a voice that displayed a considerable degree of self-confidence. 'Plans have reached an advanced stage. The "connection man" who is organising the trip says the ticket and the visa are ready. He has also booked us into a hotel. What I need is a substantial amount of US dollars to show at the immigration desk on arrival.'

'Where are you heading for?'

'Singapore.'

'Singapore?!'

'Yes, you heard me right.'

I was dumbstruck. It was no secret that many a young Ghanaian harboured the dream to travel to and settle in Aburokyire. Up till then, I knew the term was meant for destinations in the Western Industrialised world. It now seemed that the term in the meantime had been broadened to cover destinations outside the original perceived destinations!

CHAPTER 26
Tradition Gone Wild

꒰ᘓ꒱

There is a saying among the Akans in Ghana that goes like this: *Abusua do funu.* Translated, it means approximately: family members love the corpses of their departed ones. Yes, indeed, Ghanaians often go to great lengths to give their parting ones a fitting farewell to this life by way of extravagant funerals. In particular, among the majority Akans living in central and southern Ghana, the act of parting with the dead can impose a considerable financial burden on the family of the deceased.

Months, sometimes even years after the event is over, extended family members may still be struggling to repay the loans collected for this purpose. The cost of living in Ghana is high, but the cost of dying could be even higher.

The successful funeral is generally regarded by society as one that is well attended, with ample food and drink for all. Mourners dance and romp and make merry all day and night by way of loud music emanating either from powerful stereo equipment or played live by bandsmen, some being very well known musicians or performers in the country. It is not surprising that heavy expenses are incurred, necessitating loans that the mourners struggle to settle through instalments over a long period.

Many a business-orientated individual has discovered in this tendency of society to part with their dead in an exuberant manner a means of making money.

Subsequently many firms offering services that promise to make the occasion as memorable as imaginable have of late cropped up in the country. In recent times there has been intense debate at all levels of society about the need to radically reform a tradition that almost everyone agrees has got out of control. As one Member of Parliament admitted recently in a contribution to the debate, he was forced to buy thirteen different mourning clothes within a period of twelve months. Indeed, no one would have forced him to do so. He nevertheless probably saw no other option. As a prominent member of the community, he was very likely to have been watched by critical eyes whenever he turned up for such an occasion. He probably feared being branded the person who wore the same clothing or almost the same clothing wherever he went.

As a way of limiting cost and also preventing the situation where funerals are held almost every weekend, Nana and his traditional leaders have ruled that funerals are organised once in a month—in this case, the last weekend of each month. The bodies of all who die during the period are kept in the morgue at the district hospital at Goaso.

Our visit there coincided with the monthly event. The funerals are spread over the weekend beginning from Friday and lasting till late Sunday. We arrived there on a Monday evening. When we paid our usual daily visit to Rita's traditional home located in the central area of the city, my attention was drawn to the sound of sirens that reached us from time to time.

'Ghana has made significant progress," I observed. 'Now there are ambulances even in the countryside to rush the critically ill to hospital!'

'That is a wrong conclusion, Doc!' came in Papa Yaw, Rita's nephew.

'What do you mean by that?'

'They are not transporting the sick to hospital, but the dead for burial!'

'You do not mean it!'

'That is exactly the case! As you might have heard, we bury our dead and organise their funerals during the last weekend of the month. The bodies are now being brought in from the morgues at Goaso where they have been kept.'

'Why the need for the drivers to blow sirens? They are meant to facilitate the quick transfer of the critically ill to hospital. The persons who have passed away surely do not need such attention, do they?'

'Well, that is the situation. *Abusua do funu!* Maybe they do so to increase the general excitement associated with such funerals.'

'Boy, if Ghana wants to lift herself out of poverty, then this is an area we need to address. Indeed, things cannot be let to continue as it is. The government should take a lead. Admittedly government legislation cannot change the attitude of the populace overnight, but it will contribute to that.'

'In what way, Doc?'

'Well, currently there is no limit to the number of days bodies can be kept in mortuaries. The only limitation is the ability of extended family members to bear the cost. That should no longer be the case. In several countries laws are in place that specify the maximum number of days that can elapse between the time an individual dies of natural causes and the time such a person is buried. The time preceding the burial of persons who died by way of suicide, murder or through suspicious circumstances are left to the prosecuting authorities to decide.

'There is a need to introduce such legislation into the country— legislation that should not only exist in our law books, but rather should be enforced. Yes, indeed, some discipline should be introduced into the system.

'As far I am concerned seven days should be the maximum time allowed.'

'Seven days! You will hardly gain a majority for that. Take the case of prominent traditional leaders such as the Asantehene, Abuakwahene, Ga Mantse, etc! Society will want to have some time to prepare sufficiently for their burials.'

'I agree with you that such a proposal will meet initial resistance. I will not buy such an argument though! Let us cast our minds back, a hundred years or more ago, to the time when electricity had not been introduced into the country. What happened after the death of such traditional leaders? As far as I know the practice of mummification was not known to our forefathers. So what happened? Did they leave the bodies to decompose whilst they prepared for their funerals? Of course not.

'Now, thanks to someone else's invention, electricity has become available to us. What do we do with it? We use it to keep our dead bodies frozen over months—there have been instances when bodies have been kept over a year! Reason? To give the dead a fitting burial and funeral!

'Just sit down and consider it, friend. The individual is dead and gone. Only God knows where his or her spirit would be as we preserve their bodies months on end! What are we doing? Wasting energy! Yes, it boils down to a waste of energy.

'Everyone in the country seems to bemoan the current energy crisis. What are we doing with part of the precious energy generated? To freeze and conserve dead bodies!

'Another issue to consider is the financial burden it imposes on the bereaved families. It costs substantial amounts of money daily to keep the bodies in the morgues. Multiply that by the average of about three months that such bodies are usually preserved there and it amounts to a fortune!

'Another argument usually put forward to justify the need to keep the bodies over long periods of time is that several of the deceased have relations living abroad. They need time to return home to bid the dead farewell.

'I suppose that is a price we have to pay for globalisation. When my mother died thirteen years ago, I was living in Germany. I would have wished to bid her a personal farewell. Mother insisted categorically, though, that she would not want her body to be frozen after death. The extended family respected her wishes and buried her the next day. I travelled home to be part of the memorial service held a few weeks later, but I had to make do with only a video recording of the event. We cannot always have our own way in life. If governments have to take the wish of every individual in the country into account before passing necessary legislature, no progress can be made.'

'Your argument is sound. I only hope that society comes to realise the need for change.'

'It should, sooner rather than later, if we want to maintain commonsense. We should not allow ourselves to become slaves of an outdated tradition.'

It was a busy weekend indeed for residents of the town. As I learnt later, a total of fourteen bodies were buried during the time period. To ensure an orderly flow of events I learnt that the traditional councils draw up a timetable in consultation with the families concerned days ahead of the events. The time slots are not allocated arbitrarily. Instead, factors such as the religion of the departed are taken into consideration. Adherents of the SDA religion, for example, are buried on Sundays instead of Saturdays, which they consider a day of rest.

It is usually expected that residents of an area turn up to mourn with the bereaved family of the departed person who belonged to that community. There is social pressure for one to fulfil these obligations. This is particularly the case in a small community where residents are generally familiar with each other.

It was a very busy weekend indeed for residents of the town. This was particularly so owing to the fact that the celebrations were not held at a central place, but spread over various locations in the town, and this added to the stress.

One is not only expected to turn up at a funeral to condone with the relatives of a deceased person; one is also expected to make monetary donations to help meet the costs incurred. Usually such donations are recorded, making it easy for the bereaved family to establish who did not contribute. Should such a person also organise a funeral in the future, they may refuse to donate or do so after voicing their displeasure for the past omission.

'It has been a busy weekend,' Nana Kwame, one of the sub-chiefs of the traditional area, told me. 'Not only have the events exhausted me physically, they have also been a financial drain. Since I am a leading figure in the community I had to turn up at all the celebrations. Everywhere I went I was expected to make a donation— not the donation expected of an ordinary citizen but rather that which befits my status. Now, considering that about thirteen different families were involved you can imagine the financial burden—not only for this month, but every other month in the year!'

CHAPTER 27
A Doctor on a Humanitarian Mission to Ghana

꩜

At the request of Nana, I paid a courtesy call on Dr. Ahmed (name changed). As I was told, he was sent by the Ahmaddiyya Muslim Mission to man a small clinic that went into operation in the town a few weeks prior to our arrival. Desirous of setting up a mission hospital in the district, the mission went round looking for a suitable location. Eventually the decision fell on Mim; the reason being that the traditional leaders were forthcoming with land and initial accommodation for the staff.

Accompanied by the whole family, we called on Dr. Ahmed at the temporary location of the clinic. The two-storey building that previously housed the traditional council had been refurbished and converted into a waiting- and consulting- room, as well as a laboratory and a theatre for minor surgeries.

We were taken round the building by one of the newly recruited staff. 'Doc is resting at home after the morning session,' he told us and offered to take us round while we waited for his return. I noted that but for a few pieces of furniture and instruments, the building was visibly empty.

'Please take your seat in the waiting room,' he said after we had completed our tour of inspection. 'I am sure Doc will arrive at any moment.'

After we had waited for about fifteen minutes the man came back to us:

'I will go and check on him,' he said.

'Oh, do not bother him. We shall wait for a while. If he doesn't come after a while we shall call on him at another time.'

'No, I will let him know you are around. He won't be bothered if I do.' With that he left the room. He was back after a short while later.

'Doc has asked me to invite you to his home.'

'Really?'

'Yes. He said he may not be returning anytime soon, so he has asked me to take you to his home.'

The rest of the family decided to wait in the bus. I was led to a spacious detached house located almost directly opposite the clinic building on the other side of the road. A distance of about two hundred metres separated the two buildings.

A thick concrete wall surrounded the building. The metal gate led into a large paved compound. Seated on one of several chairs placed at one corner of the large open courtyard was a friendly-looking man in his late forties or early fifties. He wore a white cotton robe sewn through from top to bottom.

'Take a seat, good friend,' he began in a friendly voice.

'Thank you very much,' I replied and took a seat opposite him.

'How is the UK?'

'Well,' I smiled, 'when I left everything was fine.'

A short silence followed.

'Welcome to my premises,' he said after a while. 'Well, I have been sent to help out on the medical front here. Ghana indeed is not a new place to me,' he went on. 'All my children were born in the country. I spent several years working in one of the Ahmaddiyya Mission hospitals at Kokofu in the Ashanti region.

'In due course our mission recalled me to Pakistan. Initially I thought I was returning there for good. That was not to be the case, for hardly had I and the family settled down in our home country than I received a call to return to Ghana. I had no choice but to return. I have dedicated my life to this mission. I am always ready and happy to do to their bidding.'

As he spoke a teenage boy of about 15 emerged from the building, a tray containing two glasses filled with soft drinks in his hands. He offered one to each of us.

'Meet one of my boys,' his father smiled.

'Young man,' I asked the boy, 'how are you finding life in this town?'

'Fine thank you,' he replied in a shy voice.

Soon we were alone once again.

'I was surprised to realise on my arrival that there was not a single doctor for a town with a population of about 22000,' Dr. Ahmed continued. 'The sick have to travel ten kilometres to the district hospital at Goaso, which also boasts about the same population as this town. Even that hospital, as far as I am informed, has only a couple of doctors.' He paused for a while. 'It is a hard life here,' he continued.

'One case that was brought to my attention recently still haunts me. A man aged about thirty attended the clinic with an incarcerated hernia in his groin. Though I am competent to deal with such cases, I am at the moment not equipped with the necessary instruments to carry out the required surgery. So I decided to refer him to Goaso. Prior to that I called the colleagues there to inform them about his case. In the course of the evening, the young man showed up again—he had still not been seen by a doctor! Exasperated, I asked him and the accompanying relatives to wait while I tried to call the hospital to find out how best I could help him. Indeed, at that stage I was prepared to travel to the hospital to carry out the surgery myself. I only wanted to find out whether I would be permitted to do so and if yes, whether there would be any staff available at that time of day to assist me.

'As I was trying to sort out things in my office, I decided to return to the waiting room to check on the patient. To my utter dismay, the sick man as well as the relative accompanying him had vanished into thin air! Only God knows what happened to him.'

The conversation went on for a while thereafter. Finally I begged to leave. 'Don't forget to keep us in mind,' he told me. 'You may help us in whatever way you can. Our most pressing need at the moment is laboratory equipment that will enable us to carry out basic investigations.' He finally led me to the bus.

As I drove away I reflected on the meeting. I felt awkward, having met a foreigner on a healing mission to my country while I myself was practising my trade in an advanced country that could just as well do without me!

I did not sense a feeling of guilt, though—a moral responsibility towards improving the medical needs of my native country, yes, but a sense of guilt—no. Indeed, long before I passed out of medical school, I acquired a piece of land from the Tema Development Corporation, the state agency that administers the land of the Tema Metropolitan area with the aim of putting up a 'Christ the King Hospital' to cater for the poor and deprived of society in particular. In 1989, I launched an appeal for funds to help realise that goal. Unfortunately the response at that time was not encouraging.

At the moment I personally regard medicine not as an end in itself, but a means to an end. My main goal in life is to serve the Lord Jesus Christ who made it possible for me to study medicine in the first place. I know those who do not share my Christian faith may consider me as someone who has probably lost his mind in making such an assertion. But I stand by my words. In September 1979 my application to study medicine was turned down by the two medical schools then existing in Ghana. Eventually I was selected under the umbrella of what was then known as the Eastern Scholarships to study medicine in the then Soviet Union. Those scholarships were placed at the disposal of developing countries by the then Communist countries as a form of developing aid.

Under the scheme several students from the developing world were admitted each year to study in various institutions of higher learning in the Soviet Bloc countries. Just as I was rejoicing at the prospect of going to study there my name was eliminated from the list.

It was just about at the time of this great disappointment that the Lord sent me a vision that pointed me to Europe. Following that vision, I left Ghana in December 1980 for Nigeria to work to earn my plane ticket for Europe. After working initially on various construction sites I gained an appointment as a secondary school teacher. In the end I saved enough money to permit me to purchase a plane ticket for the then West Germany. After facing enormous problems, which culminated in a near deportation from that country, I was finally admitted to the Hannover Medical School.

I have not abandoned the idea of the *Christ the King Hospital*-- I will immediately put the plan into action should I come across the means to do so.

CHAPTER 28
On the Verge of Disaster

🙼ℂ℣

We ended our stay in Mim, on Saturday, 11th August, and headed back to Kumasi. The plan was to visit Kwasi and his family at their residence at the UST. After interacting with them for a while, we would leave to spend the night at his residence on the premises of the district hospital. The next morning we would return to Kumasi to join them in worship at their church before continuing on the same day to Mpintimpi to bid farewell to the family on our way to Accra.

There were two possible routes. The first possible route was an almost diagonal route leading south-east passing through Goaso to join the Sunyani to Kumasi road at Tepa Junction. This was the route we had used on our journey there. The alternative route would lead us 40 kilometres south to Bibiani, a town well known for its gold fields, and from there almost straight east to Kumasi, 90 kilometres away.

In the end we opted for the latter, based on the recommendation of those familiar with both routes. The latter was said not only to be in a better condition but also not as busy as the former. There was one aspect regarding the Bibian route, however, that we were warned about, viz: a few kilometres stretch of the road led through rough mountainous terrain with curves and hairpin bends at several places.

After about half an hour's drive through low-lying countryside displaying the typically green tropical vegetation, the landscape began gradually to change. Instead of flat land, several hills and mountains came into view. Corresponding with the changed landscape, the road we were travelling on, which had been straight and low-lying for the most part, increasingly began to display winding bends and arduous ascents as well as steep slopes.

Eventually we came to the bottom of a steep decline which preceded a steep rise. To facilitate the flow of traffic heading for the steep climb, the road which so far had been a single carriageway had been broadened at the base of the climb to become a dual carriageway for traffic heading towards the mountain. The dual carriageway applied only to ascending traffic.

Traffic down the slope was still by way of a single track or lane. Contrary to the situation on several roads in the country, this particular stretch of the road was visibly marked. Two bold continuous white markings were in place to underscore the need for traffic in each direction to keep to its lane.

Also clearly visible were several white arrows painted on the road to indicate the direction of traffic.

Ours was the only vehicle on the road as we began the steep climb. After driving on it for a while, I realised we were heading for a bend about a hundred metres away. The vegetation at that part of the road was thick, making it difficult for one to see beyond it. Instinctively I had all along kept to the middle lane, which happened to be a direct extension of the lane I had all along been driving on. Barely a few metres before the bend, something in me told me to abandon the middle lane for the outside one. No sooner had I done so than I witnessed something which to this day continues to baffle my imagination. All of a sudden, and as if from nowhere, a large tipper truck emerged from the sharp bend a few metres ahead of us, driving—incredibly—in the middle lane, the lane that was absolutely out of bounds for traffic coming in that direction!

Even to this day, I cannot fathom what it was that led the driver to use that lane. His action was completely unprovoked. There was no impediment in his way, he was not being hassled by any pursuing vehicle, and the lane earmarked for his use was completely free. So why did he choose to place the lives of others in such danger?

Indeed, I just could not imagine what would have happened to us in the event that I hadn't changed lanes seconds before! One thing is certain, however—there would have been little chance of escape! I would probably have instinctively swerved to the side, lost control of the vehicle in the process, and been powerless to prevent it from rolling over several times down the steep slope and finally crashing into the valley below. Or, had I been left with no time to swerve, we might have crashed head on into the huge truck. It is anyone's guess what would have remained of a Mercedes mini-bus and its occupants after crashing into a truck not only of its size but against the momentum of its own mass, combined with the force of gravity pulling us down the steep slope.

My driving school instructor used to say that a driver on the road is exposed to three hazards—firstly the hazards that could result from the mistakes committed by himself/herself, secondly the hazards that could result from defects of the vehicle, and lastly hazards that could result from the mistakes committed by a third party. Whereas the driver can have some control over the first two factors, he or she is powerless in regard to the third.

I have made it a habit, always when I set out on a journey, to say a silent prayer for the Lord of heaven and earth to preserve me and the occupants of my vehicle on the road.

I do not know what the reader will make of the story just told. Will he/she ascribe the escape to chance? For me, however, there was no doubt in my mind that we were preserved only by the protecting arm of the Lord of heaven and earth.

We arrived safely in Kumasi without any further incidents. After asking our way a couple of times we were finally directed to the residence of Kwasi and his family on the premises of the Kwame Nkrumah University of Science and Technology, around 15:00 hrs.

CHAPTER 29
A Pleasant Re-union

W e were heartily welcomed by Kwasi and Georgina into their home. When I last saw them in 1991, they had two children. In the meantime the number had increased to four. I could hardly recognise the two little children I met sixteen years before. Their first child, who was about four at that time, had developed into an attractive young woman whereas the boy, who at that time was only a few months old, had developed into a well-built teenager bubbling with energy.

Kind-hearted Georgina had taken so much trouble to prepare a sumptuous dinner of jolof rice and fried chicken! To her disappointment, however, we could eat only a small portion of what we were offered. Over the last few days I had been plagued with traveller's diarrhoea that had not only sapped my energy, but had robbed me of my appetite. Regarding the rest of the family, the scorching heat had made them drink a considerable amount of water during the drive from Mim.

As we chatted about various issues, it suddenly occurred to me that Kwasi had told me in a previous conversation about Georgina's three-month stay in Singapore. Indeed, she had returned only a few weeks prior to our arrival in the country. According to him, she was there to attend a seminar on church leadership. I decided to take advantage of the insights she might have gained while there to find out what she thought about the prospect of an unskilled immigrant from Ghana finding meaningful employment in Singapore.

'Doc,' she smiled, 'sometimes I marvel at the kind of stuff some of our people are made up of! Many of our citizens have taken advantage of the fact that one normally does not need a visa to enter that country.'

'Did I hear you right, that one does not require a visa to get there?'

'Yes, that is the case. I think the authorities want to maintain the country's reputation as a tourist haven. As a result they do not demand visas from those arriving in the country. One has to produce enough hard currency on arrival, though, to convince them one is capable of sustaining oneself during the stay.'

At that moment, I remembered the conversation I had with the woman and her son, during which they talked about having invested money to acquire a visa. Poor them! I could imagine the 'connection man' demanding a considerable sum of money from them with the aim of procuring a visa for Singapore!

'Somehow,' she continued, 'some of our citizens got to know about the liberal entry requirements of that place. Before long they began to pour into that country.'

'Is it easy for an unskilled foreigner to find employment there?' I still wanted to know.

'I shouldn't think it would be easy. I know they have stringent requirements in place making it very difficult for one who arrives there from the outside to gain employment. Those Ghanaians who arrived there at the beginning of the influx, on realising how difficult it was to find work in Singapore, continued on to Malaysia where the prospects of finding work seemed better. At first the Malaysian authorities allowed them in without demanding any visas. As the number of new arrivals from this West African country soared, however, the authorities reacted by requiring them to obtain visas before being allowed to enter.'

At that juncture I told her about the young man from Mim who was sitting on his packed baggage about to leave for that country.

'As far as Singapore is concerned, there is *no way* he can find work!' she said emphatically. 'With some luck, he may find something to do in Malaysia. But he must first make it there. I doubt, though, whether he will manage to obtain a visa that will enable him to cross over.'

It wouldn't take long for her prediction to become reality. One evening, about four weeks after our return to the UK, I had just returned home from a busy day's work when our phone rang. I picked up the phone and was greeted by the voice of one of Rita's relations at Mim. The concern in her voice was apparent.

'What is the matter?' I asked.

'Maame Afia, the woman who sold her piece of cocoa farm to you, is here with me; she wants to speak to you.'

'What is the matter?' I wanted to know.

'You speak to her yourself,' she replied.

'Good evening Doc,' her voice came over the phone. 'I need your urgent help!'

'Yet another time!'

'Yes indeed.'

'What is the matter?'

'My son is stranded in Singapore!'

'That cannot be true.'

'Yes indeed, he called a few hours ago. According to him, he as well as two other Ghanaians he is travelling with have run out of money. They have had nothing to eat for three days, he says. He is urgently appealing to me to remit them some money without delay to enable them to move on to Malaysia, where, according to him, they stand a chance of gaining employment. I tried to do so through the Western Union at Mim. They told me that due to technical reasons they are not in a position to carry out that transaction. So I am calling to find out whether you can do the transaction from your end. The amount involved is US$1500. You can deduct the amount from what you owe me from the sale of the farm.'

I readily offered to help, at which she provided me with his contact number in Singapore. Owing to the time difference I said I would wait till the next day before making contact with him.

'No please, call him *now* please,' she urged. 'He says he has not been able to sleep for days! The assurance that the money will be reaching him tomorrow will give him peace of mind and enable him to sleep.'

'Okay, I will do that.'

Moments later I was dialling Singapore. After I introduced myself, I got straight to the point. His mother had requested me to transfer US$1500 to him. He should expect it the next day.

'Could you please make it US$2000!' he pleaded. 'We are travelling in a group of three. I cannot leave the other two stranded.'

A selfless fellow, I thought. Even with his problem he had the welfare of others at heart.

'Well, that is your mother's money. You have to confirm this with her when you call her.'

I made the transaction the next day as agreed. Matters did not end there, however. About two weeks later we received another call from his mother. They had eventually made it to Shanghai! Fortunately, they had found another Ghanaian who was trying to assist them. He had permitted them to stay with him in a small room the hotel he was working for had placed at his disposal. He needed US$1000 to be able to process his working permit. She was appealing to me to use the last instalment of the money I owed her for this purpose. I obliged and carried out the transaction without delay.

If only matters would end there! A few days later Rita's relation rang to tell me the lady wanted to speak to me in the evening. She wanted to find out from me whether I would be able to send some money to her son on her behalf. I replied by saying that I would only do so if she handed the cedi equivalent of the money involved to a trusted person in Ghana. I have since not heard from her.

One can only wonder at the tendency of so many Ghanaians to look abroad for prospects of making it in life when in reality there are many opportunities at home to do so.

I overheard someone relating a story to another person during my stay in Ghana. The person who was telling the story said he was working for a Syrian national who had moved into the country to set up a business enterprise.

'I am perplexed at what I have observed in this country since my arrival,' he was reported to have said.

'What have you observed?' one of his employees inquired.

'I am surprised to find so many Ghanaians travelling abroad in search of greener pastures, when indeed there is immense opportunity here to make money.'

CHAPTER 30
Blessed are the Meek …

T he next day we packed all our items back into the bus and returned to Kumasi to meet Kwasi and his family at an agreed location near their Church, the Calvary Charismatic Church, to join them in worship. Ghanaians are very religious. Presently the majority of residents, particularly those in central and southern Ghana, ascribe to the Christian faith. Next in line is Islam, which is prominent in the north. A small minority adhere to various forms of traditional African religious beliefs.

Situated near the Airport roundabout in central Kumasi, the church boasts a large congregation. According to Kwasi, as a result of that, it is forced to hold three Sunday morning services. We attended the third one. The attendance was good, the large church building filled almost to capacity. We were told that the same thing applied to the two earlier services.

Judging from the outfits of those attending as well as the cars they were driving, the church might as well be located anywhere in the US— another example of the first world colliding with the third in Ghana. Pastor Ransford Obeng, founder and head pastor of the Church, made a good impression on me. Notwithstanding the size of his congregation and the popularity the church had gained in the area, the impression he made on me was that of a simple, modest and down-to-earth personality.

His attitude contrasted greatly with another church we visited during our stay. On that occasion the pastor, who was introduced to the congregation with the title Professor (I wondered which University had conferred that title on him), claimed to have the power to heal all diseases, help all become successful in their business transactions, help all looking for partners find one, help all wishing to settle in Aburokyire to do so.... the list of all that he was capable of doing was endless!

To my surprise the large church was packed to the very last seat. For each problem he prayed for, monetary donations was demanded. At the end of the service he drove away in his posh 4x4 Toyota Landcruiser V8.

His was not an isolated case, Kwasi told me. There has been a proliferation of such feel-good preachers in the country. They have been fostered in the main by the poor and needy of society looking for quick solutions to the problems plaguing them, be they improvements in their living situations or short-cut to wealth.

These preachers, instead of making the salvation message the core of their preaching, wealth and how to attain it in the shortest possible time has assumed prominence in their feel-good, quick-fix messages.

CHAPTER 31
The Driving Cousin

W e bade a final farewell to Kwasi and his family after the service which lasted till about 13:00 hrs and headed southwards, to Mpintimpi, to bid farewell to Father and the relations. Our plan was to spend two days there. From there we would continue on to Amantia, mother's hometown to spend a night. Our final stop before finally returning to Accra to await our flight back to Europe would be at Akim Oda, the district capital about forty kilometres to the south of Amantia; the plan was to spend a night there.

As expected, Father, the extended family and all the residents of the village were delighted to welcome us. I shall spare readers the trouble of having to read an account of our second stay at my place of birth since it will amount almost to a repetition of what they already know from our first.

Worthy of mention perhaps are two things. Several relations of mine living elsewhere in the country, who had not been aware of our first visit, on hearing about our impending second visit took pains to travel, in some cases considerable distances, to the village to greet us.

We did not stay at Nkawkaw on this occasion, but rather at Afosu, a small town about seven kilometres to the south of the village. The town where I had part of my elementary education had expanded considerably over the years. A few well-to-do citizens there had in the meantime put up a handful of hotels and guesthouses of commendable quality. It was in one of these guesthouses that we spent the two nights of our stay.

We left Afosu in the very early hours of Tuesday, 14th August to travel to Amantia. Due to problems finding suitable accommodation in the area, we decided not to spend the night there. Instead we would interact with members of the extended family resident there during the day and leave before nightfall.

News had reached us the previous night to warn us about the poor state of the road leading to the village. The untarred road, we were told, had been rendered almost impassable by torrential rains of the past few days. On hearing that, one of my cousins who, since his childhood had been fascinated with automobiles and who had become known by the alias *Kwaku Driver,* offered to drive us there. It was a kind gesture on his part, considering that he would have to rest his own *tro-tro* which he plied between Mpintimpi and Nkawkaw for the day.

Due to his long experience driving on such roads, he managed to drive us safely to our destination. The first thing we did on reaching my late mother' s hometown was to visit her grave as well as that of Emmanuel, my eldest brother, who passed away thirteen years before her.

As I had expected, we were accorded a rousing welcome, not only by my extended family members but also by almost all the residents of the little town who had not yet left for work on their farms. They were disappointed however when they learnt that we would not be spending the night there.

CHAPTER 32
Stuck on the Birim River

W e ended our visit to Amantia at aroud 16:00 hrs and headed for
Akim Oda about forty kilometres to the south. Kwaku Driver
handed over the responsibility of steering the vehicle back to me when
we got to Ofoase, a larger town about five kilometres to the south of
Amantia. It happens to be located on the main road linking the two main
towns in the area Nkawkaw and Akim Oda. He did not have to wait long
after alighting from our vehicle to continue his journey, for a passenger
vehicle heading for Nkawkaw soon pulled to a stop.

Akim Oda, the capital of the Akim Kotoku district, occupies an
important place in my personal biography. It was namely at the Akim
Oda Secondary School that I completed my secondary education.
Moving from the village Mpintimpi to attend the boarding school at
Oda was to me like moving from a beggar's hut to dwell in a king's
palace. Henceforth, at least during the time when school was in session,
I would enjoy the privilege of drinking clean water, having access to
electricity, watching TV and enjoying three regular and delicious meals
daily with the luxury of cutlery!

One might understand why I was proud to show my children my
Alma Mater, even if the time available to us would not permit anything
else apart from pointing it out to them from a distance.

Our plan was to spend the night at a hotel yet to be identified there.
The next day I would pay a surprise visit to Akwasi, a good old friend
of mine who gave me financial assistance during a critical stage of my
sixth form education, for which kind gesture I am eternally grateful.

There was also a 'social packet' in my pocket for a resident of the town. Nana Kwame, the eldest son of Afia, the nephew at Amantia who boasted ten children, needed my assistance. He was about to complete an apprenticeship in carpentry. Several months before our departure for Ghana from the UK he had called to request financial assistance to enable him to purchase a wood-spraying machine he needed for his trade. His market research had revealed he would need the equivalent of about 200 dollars for the purpose. The plan was to pick him up the next day and travel with him to Accra. There I would accompany him to an area of the city where the machines are on sale and purchase one for him. He would return to Oda the same day to use the machine in building up his living.

Contrary to our expectations, we made good progress on our way. The stretch of road leading from Akim Ofoase to Akim Oda, which in times past had gained notoriety among those who had to use it for being in a chronically bad state, had in the meantime been renovated and tarred.

About halfway through the journey, Rita came up with a suggestion.

'At the rate at which we are progressing we would be well advised to consider heading straight to Accra instead of making a stopover in Akim Oda. That would spare us not only the burden of going in search of a suitable hotel there, but also of having to unpack all our luggage tonight only to repack it again early tomorrow morning!'

'That's a good idea. As far as my visit to Akwasi is concerned, I could postpone it to a future date. Concerning Nana Kwame, we could arrange for him to meet us in Accra at another time.'

'Don't forget the matter of accommodation,' Karen, who had been following events, joined in. 'Where shall we sleep when we arrive in Accra tonight?' She was indeed right, for Lena's Inn was expecting us the next day, and not that evening.

'We just have to call them and make our intentions known to them. I am sure they will find somewhere for us tonight,' Rita suggested. 'Otherwise we shall spend the night in the bus!'

'If push comes to shove we will have to. I hope however we do not have to!'

'There is still another problem—we do not have the number of the hotel. We left the leaflet containing it at the hotel.'

'No problem. All we need to do is call Kwasi and request him to pass the message on.'

Soon Karen was busy with her mobile phone, trying to tease out his number. Moments later she was through to him. On hearing what she had to say, he promised to do as requested.

Not long afterwards, on the left side of the road, the predominantly white building blocks on the large compound of the Oda Secondary School came into view in the distance.

As we passed it, I proudly pointed out my Alma Mater to the rest of the family.

We needed to travel about ten kilometres to reach the town. From there we still needed to travel a distance of about 90 kilometres to reach our destination.

The next important landmark on our way to Oda was the Birim River, one of the major rivers in the country, well known for the rich deposits of diamonds along its basins. Indeed, Akwatia, a town situated near the Birim River to the south-east of Oda, boasts the largest diamond mines in the country.

A large metal bridge spans the river to facilitate both vehicular and rail transport. Just across the bridge is found a large wood-processing factory, Oda Sawnmills Ltd which draws its raw material from the abundant wood in the tropical rain forests in the area.

Just as we were nearing the bridge, we negotiated a bend only to be confronted by a young man who stood by the wayside about one hundred metres from us, waving a branch of a tree he held in one hand, gesticulating for us to stop. I noticed that a queue of vehicles had built up in the distance.

'What is the matter?' I inquired from the young man whose age I put at about thirty.

'Unfortunately, sir, there is no going forward.'

'Why not?'

'A large truck loaded with several logs of wood is stuck on the bridge, just halfway between the two ends. The lorry is so broad, nothing apart from perhaps a bike, can pass it where it is!'

'The middle of the Birim bridge: not a suitable place for a vehicle to break down!'

'It is not broken down, sir! At least, not in the strictest sense of the word.'

'What do you mean, friend?'

'It sounds incredible yet it is true—the truck ran out of diesel just as it got to the very middle of the bridge!'

'That cannot be true!'

'Massa, I tell you this is the situation we live with! Some of these trucks are not fit for the road, especially so when they have to transport dangerous loads such as huge tropical trees. Yet they are still plying the roads. In this case, I am sure the fuel indicator stopped working long, long ago. Yet no one took the pains to have it repaired!'

'How long do you think we'll have to wait here?'

'It could be several hours!'

'You don't meant it!'

'That unfortunately is the situation. My understanding is that the truck belongs to a company in town. The driver has left for their office at the centre of town to complete the necessary paperwork that would lead to the release of funds for the acquisition of the needed fuel. That could take hours, sir. Who knows whether he will even meet the responsible person at the office at this time of day.'

'That is harsh.'

'Where are you heading for?'

'Accra.'

'You do not have to wait that long here. Fortunately for you there is an alternate route that begins not far from here.'

'How can I find it?'

'I will direct you. You turn and follow the road from where you came. About one kilometre from here you will meet a branch road to your right. Turn into it and follow it. It will take you to Kade. From there you can continue on to your destination. I want to warn you, though— the road leading to Kade is in a poor state. From there onwards, it is okay—all the way to Accra.'

We decided to take the risk and drive through Kade instead of wait for the truck driver to return with his fuel. Where was the guarantee that he would be returning any sooner?

The stranger was right concerning his warning as to the poor state of the road leading from the junction to Kade. The approximately forty-kilometre stretch of road was untarred, had a rugged surface and due to recent heavy downpours of rain, was muddy and in several places filled with ponds of water.

After we had travelled about ten kilometres along it the road came to a sharp curve. The scene that confronted me after the bend sent cold shivers down my spine.

About one hundred metres ahead of us, a large truck loaded with three large timber trees travelling in the direction we were coming from was standing in the middle of the road! The road at that point was narrow, making it impossible to overtake it.

'My goodness, yet another broken down timber truck!' I yelled and pulled the vehicle to a stop a few metres away from the hindrance.

We soon discovered that the vehicle was not abandoned. Instead three men were at work trying to fasten a strong metal chain to the huge logs of wood loaded unto it.

'Has your vehicle broken down, friends?' I inquired nervously.

'No, we are okay!'

'What are you up to then?'

'We stopped to offer assistance to the saloon car behind us. got stuck in the mud.' (The truck had until then blocked the car from our view.) 'The job having been done, we are preparing to resume our journey. We are in the process of fastening the chain we employed to pull the vehicle from the mud back into place.'

As he spoke we saw the vehicle helped out of the mud pull away, heading in the direction we were travelling.

'Do you think we can make it past the spot where the other vehicle got stuck?' I wanted to know.

'Definitely. Yours is equipped with a more powerful engine. Put it in first gear and don't commit the mistake the other driver made by trying to avoid the pond in the middle of the road. The underlying earth is solid, not like the earth that borders it—that is mud, thick slippery mud.'

We needed to overcome one immediate hurdle though, namely how to get our vehicles past each other at that narrow stretch of road.

After consulting with each other we came up with a plan. I would reverse my vehicle over a distance of about fifty metres to a spot where the road was broad enough to permit both vehicles to pass each other. I would wait on the side of the road that would normally be used by oncoming traffic.

The truck would then drive slowly past by using the space so created. For that brief moment at least we would be putting the traffic regulations of the country, which requires vehicles to drive on the right side of the road, out of use.

Soon we set out to put our plans into action. After I had positioned myself at the agreed location, the truck driver set his vehicle in motion. Slowly and with much caution he moved the huge vehicle towards us. As he got to where we were we waved each other goodbye.

'Dont forget my advice!' he called out to me. 'Put the vehicle in first gear and drive straight through the pond of water with all the force the engine can muster. Good luck!'

He waved with a broad smile as he drove slowly past. I started my engine, engaged first gear and with my right foot pressing firmly on the accelerator, drove through the middle of the pond as advised.

'We have made it!' we all screamed in delight as we put the hindrance behind us.

The area through which we then drove is a part of the country known for its palm plantations. Over a long stretch on both sides of the road we could only see lines of palm trees, as far as the eye could see. I wondered though why the road leading to such an important commercial area should be left in that poor state.

After about an hour's drive on that rugged road through the quiet countryside we reached the outskirts of Kade which lies about 110 kilometres to the northwest of Accra. As we neared it, memories of my last visit there several years ago came to mind. Afosu, where I registered to take the so-called Common Entrance Examination of the West African Examinations Council, which eventually opened the way for me to be admitted to the Oda Secondary School, did not boast an exams centre. As a result I had to travel about seventy kilometres to the centre at Kade.

CHAPTER 33
Mosquito Coils for Night Duty

A s we got to the outskirts of the town we were confronted by a scene that had in the meantime become very familiar to us—a police checkpoint. A young officer armed with a long-barrelled gun approached our vehicle.

'Where are you heading for?' he inquired.

'Accra,' I replied.

'Have you got something for me? I mean, something that will enable me to purchase a mosquito coil?'

'Didn't the person who posted you here provide for that?'

'No sir!' he replied, a broad smile on his face. I dipped my hand into the bag containing our money, pulled out a few freshly printed one Ghana cedi notes and handed them to him.

'Thank you very much and may God bless you!'

Soon we were on our way. Having been in the country for a while and having realised how high the cost of living was, I no longer regarded such deeds as bribery and corruption but rather as voluntary handouts to help others make ends meet.

Another incident worthy of mention would soon follow.

After pulling a few kilometres away from the said checkpoint, we had to stop because of a queue of vehicles that had built up before us. From the distance where we were we could make out a couple of police officers.

'Yet another checkpoint!' I told the rest.

'But we just passed one!' Rita remarked.

'Well, they seem to be everywhere,' I added.

One by one the vehicles ahead of me moved forward, pulling to a halt at a wooden structure in the middle of the road that separated traffic from either side of the road. About twenty metres from the structure, a few policemen were still conducting checks on some of the vehicles that had just stopped at what I initially took to be a checkpoint.

Soon our vehicle stood at the head of the queue. Unfamiliar with what was going on, I decided to wait until the police officer signalled me to proceed. Before long the driver behind me was blowing his horn loudly. Initially, I could not make any sense of it—after all, sounding the horn of a vehicle is nothing strange in my native Ghana; in effect, one could call it a kind of national sport! This time, however, I sensed something behind it, for the young man at the wheel of the Nissan Urvan mini-bus filled to the last seat with commuters was not only sounding his horn but also screaming and shouting insults at me.

'Hey driver, why are you standing there! Move on, you drunkard!' I did not move but waited calmly for the police officer to signal me to proceed.

"Hey, policeman, you better arrest him for drink driving!' my fellow motorist shouted. 'He must be drunk!'

In the meantime some of the passengers had also become aggressive and began shouting insults at the 'drink and drive' driver! In the confusion one word emanating from the furious passengers came clearly through: 'Toll, toll, toll!'

'Get out and check for yourself,' Rita urged me. 'It seems to be a toll road.' I got out and walked ahead to find things out for myself, something which infuriated the driver and passengers behind me even further.

Soon the reality came home to me: the wooden structure was indeed a tollbooth, operating independently of the neighbouring police checkpoint! For those drivers using the road on almost a daily basis it was familiar spot. How did they expect a stranger to know this when there was no sign anywhere pointing to it?

As I returned to the vehicle after having paid my bill, the driver and a considerable number of the passengers continued to hurl insults at me. As I drove on, the police officer signalled me and minutes later the driver of the Nissan Urvan to stop. The driver behind me initially followed the order, but on noticing that the officers had directed their attention at me, he set his vehicle in motion and sped away from the scene!

'Let him go,' one of the officers told his colleague. 'We shall get him tomorrow!' Then he turned his attention to me. 'Your driving licence please,' he demanded

Without uttering a word, I handed him my UK licence.

On noticing the country of issue one of the officers turned to me and inquired: 'In which Inverness do you live?'

'Pardon?' I asked

'I mean, in which Inverness do you live?'

Inverness? I asked myself. What did he mean by that? Although I had lived in the UK only eighteen months and did not have a detailed knowledge of its geography, the little knowledge I possessed told me Inverness was a city in the Scottish Highlands! Did he mean which home nation or probably which county I lived in?

'I do not know what you mean by your question,' I began. 'It may interest you to know, however, that I live in England, in the English Midlands.'

'Do you have some pounds for us—£100 perhaps?'

Even his colleague was clearly taken aback by his question.

'Do you know the equivalent of a hundred pounds in our currency, friend? It is approximately 1.8 million cedis! So, friend, let us ask for something reasonable!'

'Na Masa from Aburokyire, you just give us some pocket money. We need to feed our children.'

I reached for my bag and handed them four newly printed Ghana cedi notes.

'For your children, mind you!' I said.

'Thank you very much—they will be grateful.'

As we moved on, I began to wonder what the toll being collected was for, for there was no difference in the state of the road before and after the booth—it was still single carriage and displayed the same characteristics as the one that preceded the booth; neither was there any unusual construction, a hanging bridge, for example, the financing of which needed to be repaid in some way.

The rest of our journey was uneventful. Finally, at approximately 22:00 hrs we pulled up at the gates of Lena's Inn. The effect of travelling along the stretch of road from the junction to Kade was everywhere evident on our vehicle—it looked as if it had been immersed from the wheels to the door handles in a pond of mud. Junior, bless him, had not left the duty of welcoming us to his workers but had rather kept watch waiting for us. As promised, we were privileged this time to stay in the self-catering property.

It was a marked difference from the ordinary hotel rooms—we had a large fully furnished hall boasting satellite TV and a large fridge as well as two large bedrooms, a well equipped spacious kitchen as well as a neat bath and toilet facilities at our disposal.

CHAPTER 34
The African Queen who Collapsed on Enthronement

I was awakened the next morning by the ringing of my mobile phone. Who, I wondered, was calling at that early hour of the day? It turned out to be Afia Ampong, the widow of my late brother Emmanuel. Though he had passed away about a quarter of a century ago, she has maintained a close relationship with his family members.

'I heard you were back in Accra,' she said. 'I called to find out about your plans for today: I am planning to prepare you some meals.'

That was typical Afia; on all occasions that I have been in Ghana she has gone to generous measures in her hospitality.

'We may be in town to do some shopping but shall be back home by the late afternoon.'

'Is it okay to call on you around 17:00 hrs?'

'That will be fine.'

'Okay, expect us around that time. I will be coming with all your three daughters.' (In our culture the daughters of my brother are not regarded as my nieces but as my own children.)

Just as I was about to end the call, her voice reached me again.

'I almost forgot to tell you something.'

'What then?'

'About the dramatic experience Adwoa went through three days ago.'

'What happened?'

'We nearly lost one of our grandchildren,' she continued.

'You do not mean it!'

'Yes I do! It involved one of the daughters of Adwoa. She was out playing with her friends when all of a sudden one of them rushed to her mother shouting:

"Come and see, Akosua is no longer talking!" Adwoa rushed out to ascertain what was wrong with her seven-year-old daughter. She found her lying unconscious on the field where they had been playing, much of her hair covered with a white powdery substance! In panic, she cried out her name and shook her several times in a desperate attempt to revive her—to no avail.

'What was to be done? There was no hospital around. Could she look out for a taxi to drive her along the congested streets to Korle Bu? That would take her at least an hour, she reasoned. In her desperation, an idea occurred to her—to take her to the pastor of her church who happened to live in the neighbourhood to be prayed for. Fortunately he was at home. He did not hesitate a moment but began immediately to call on the name of the Lord for help.

'After praying fervently for several minutes the miracle happened— the unconscious girl suddenly regained consciousness!'

'That is amazing!'

'It was indeed a miracle. Everybody witnessing it began to shout and were jubilant on account of the incredible happening.'

'How is she now?'

'She is fine. She will accompany us on the visit.'

'How did the white substance get into her hair?'

'She was playing on a field not far from their home with her friends when they came across a white substance wrapped into a ball by means of a transparent polythene bag. Since it was transparent, it revealed the substance contained in it—a white powdery substance. Out of curiosity, they decided to give it a closer look.

Thinking that it was ordinary talcum powder one of them said:

"'I have an idea!"

"'What idea?" they asked as if with one voice.

"'Why not crown Akosua queen of the group by pouring the powder on her head!" (The crowing of traditional leaders in Ghana comes to a climax with the pouring of white powder on their heads.)

"'That is a good idea!" the rest shouted in unison.

'Soon they put their plan into action and poured the contents of the plastic bag over her head. Shortly afterwards she collapsed and lost consciousness.

'Surprised that their "newly-crowned queen" was no longer responding, they ran for help.'

'Did they send a sample of the substance to the police?'

'No,'

'Why not? Investigation should have been conducted to ascertain what kind of stuff was involved.'

'That idea certainly did not cross their minds. What was important to them was the restoration of the sick.'

CHAPTER 35
Braving the Odds to Success

I f there was any individual in the country aside from our close relatives and a few close friends we were keen to meet, it was surely Eddie. He is a person I accord the greatest respect; not because he has risen to become one of the leading producers of pineapple in the country but because of the path he trod to attain that feat.

I first heard about him in the summer of 2004. That was when I was travelling with Eric, a close associate of mine, to attend a gathering of Ghanaians in Germany in Wiesbaden, near Frankfurt. As Eric sat on the passenger seat beside me his mobile phone began to ring. A lively conversation followed that lasted for more than half an hour. From what I got to hear, I gathered that the call came from Ghana.

'Who is that who can afford to spend such long time on a call from Ghana?' I inquired when the conversation was over.

'That's peanuts to him!'

'Really?'

'Yes, indeed.'

'Who is he, then? A leading politician perhaps?'

'No, a farmer.'

'A farmer?'

'Yes, a prominent one for that matter—one of the leading exporters of pineapples in the country.'

'Really?'

'Every week he charters a cargo plane to transport his pineapples to Europe.'

'He must be earning good money!'

'Yes, he has certainly made it. The way he got there is a fairy tale story. After his graduation from the University he was posted to the Ministry of Trade to do his national service. Whilst there he came across letters from Europeans dealing in pineapples. They inquired about the possibility of finding local farmers who could supply them with commercial quantities of the fruit on a regular basis.

'His superior seemed uninterested in the topic, for whenever they passed the letters on to him, they instructed him to file them away without any action being taken. As the queries kept on coming an idea occurred to him—write down the respective addresses of the senders for possible future use.

'In due time, he ended his national service and gained employment with one of the leading financial institutions in the country. Even while he worked for the financial institution, the correspondence with the potential pineapple purchasers in Europe continued to haunt him.

'Eventually he made a decision which was as shock to many—to resign his secure and comfortable position at the bank and venture into pineapple farming!

'On hearing this, his father nearly exploded in anger.

'"I have sacrificed resources to educate you up to university level for you only to become a farmer!" he burst out. "Why didn't you make your intentions known to me at the beginning, rather than wait until I had invested a fortune in your education!"

'I can understand the sentiments expressed by his father,' I put in. 'A banker going into agriculture—in a society where even those with degrees in agriculture rarely leave the comfort of their office for the field!'

'Don't blame them, my friend. Anyone of them who dares do so can expect a similar reaction from their relatives and friends. The average person at home cannot just associate education, and for that matter university education with farming.'

'Indeed, we have a serious social problem, my friend!'

'Education, education, education! That is what hopefully will bring about a change in attitude.'

'We need that urgently, friend.'

'Well, allow me to finish my story. For his decision to go into farming, he was alienated by the rest of his extended family.'

'Oh, really!'

'Yes. Whenever something important concerning the family needed to be discussed no one bothered to invite him. He was not perturbed, however. Instead he persisted in his goal, not allowing what others thought or said about him distract him from his course. With the little capital that he could lay hands on he acquired a piece of land and began to execute his plan.

'Owing to his limited resources, initially, he had to do a great deal of the work himself. During the daytime he cleared the land and grew the young plants; in the evenings he could be seen carrying a bucket of water on his way to water the plants.

'Gradually, his efforts began to bear fruit as his plantation began to flourish. In due course he was harvesting the fruits in commercial quantities. Armed with the addresses he acquired during his time at the Trade Ministry, he went about looking for European trading partners.'

'How did his father and other relatives react to the new situation?'

'In utter disbelief, in utter disbelief! In the end they appealed to some respected members of the community to help bring about a reconciliation. That has in the meantime happened.'

'That is a story worthy to broadcast to the ears of everyone back home in Ghana. Indeed, we need to discard the notion that farming is not for the educated. In Europe and elsewhere, for example, one might come across an agricultural graduate driving his own tractor, working on his own farm.

'Not so in Ghana. People go to the university and other institutions of higher learning to acquire knowledge and other techniques of farming only to barricade themselves within the comforts of their offices, leaving the illiterate farmers to do the actual farming. It is high time, indeed, that we discarded the notion that farming is not for the educated.'

Not long after the above conversation, we had the opportunity of meeting the atypical Ghanaian farmer personally in Düsseldorf. He had made a stop in Germany on a business trip to Europe. Thereafter we maintained the contact by way of occasional telephone calls.

Not only Rita and myself were desirous of meeting him; the children were as well, if only for a different reason—they yearned to see a pineapple plantation at first hand and also enjoy a ripe pineapple harvested directly from the source. Finding a time to meet that suited both parties proved difficult, mainly because of his heavy schedule and also partly because of our visit to the countryside. An opportunity finally presented itself on 16th August, exactly a week prior to our departure.

After missing our way a couple of times we finally located the farm, situated about fifty kilometres to the west of Accra.

The first thing that attracted our attention was a huge metal building measuring about fifty metres in length and thirty metres in breadth. It stood about ten metres above the surface of the cemented hall. It was roofed by way of corrugated aluminium sheets. Near the entrance of the building several workers were busily loading a large lorry with boxes packed with pineapples. As we were later told, they would be transported to the harbour or the airport for further transport to Europe.

One of the workers signalled for us to follow him. Just then we caught sight of our guest, Eddy, seated in the open about a hundred metres away. Just near him several chairs had been placed around a large table. About ten metres from where he sat two men were gathered around a barbeque, busily at work grilling several pieces of steak spread on top of the rack.

We were warmly received by our host who recounted with joy some of the memorable moments of our last meeting in Germany. Just as we were engaged in the hearty exchange a young woman whose age I put at about twenty emerged from the main building, a large tray containing drinks and cups in her hands.

After serving us the drinks she returned to where she had come only to reappear moments later carrying a tray which this time contained plates and sets of cutlery. After a few more comings and goings, our meal of rice, yams, sauce and several pieces of delicious-looking steaks was ready to be enjoyed.

'What type of meat is that?' Karen asked curiously.

'Akrante.'

'What is akrante?

'Grasscutter.'

'Grasscutter?'

'Yes, it is a very popular meat in Ghana. Your parents can testify to that.'

'Did you order it specially for us?'

'No, we rear them here—over there,' he replied, pointing to a large wooden structure about seventy metres from where we were seated. 'We keep not only grasscutters; we have goats as well as poultry.'

'So you do not grow only pineapples but produce livestock as well?'

'The pineapples provide for my livelihood; rearing animals is a hobby that has helped make me almost independent of the meat market!'

'Am I permitted to have a look at the animals?' Who else but Jonathan would express such a wish!

'Yes, of course, but be patient and let us finish the meal first.' As we enjoyed our meal, I took the opportunity to discuss some of the developments I had observed since our arrival.

'I noticed Accra has become terribly congested compared to the way it used to be thirteen years ago,' I began.

'Not only has it become congested,' our host expanded, 'it is also overrun with thieves, rogues, pickpockets and what have you!

'The situation should not come as a surprise to anyone. What else can one expect of a multitude of semi-educated and unskilled people who have thronged the capital in search of non-existent jobs?

'The attitude of the youth of this generation beats my understanding, my friend. Many of them want to become rich within the shortest possible time without shedding any sweat in return. Instead of staying in the countryside to engage in farming the way our parents did, they have flocked to the towns and cities.

'And what about those who stay behind? They remain idle, leaving the aged to do the farming. If only the story would end there, but no. The moment the crops produced by the frail and aged reach maturity they see their chance and go under the cover of darkness to steal them!

'I do not know what the future holds for our country should that attitude continue unchecked.'

At that juncture, I decided to inform him about the land I had acquired for the purpose of farming.

'It is a good idea, my friend. Still, I do see danger ahead. Yes, I personally do not believe in what I term absentee-farming. Indeed, you may send money on a regular basis to meet the cost of labour and other inputs. Whether the money sent is utilised for the purpose for which it was meant is another question. I warn you, friend—in the present-day Ghana hardly anyone can be entrusted with money. Indeed, not even your close relatives and friends can be exempted.'

'What in your opinion has led to this situation?'

'In my opinion two factors could be cited—the high cost of living on one hand and the abundance of goods on the market on the other. In former times the goods were not available: now they are available but being sold at prices beyond the reach of many. Those unable to resist the temptation to live above their means resort to crooked means to satisfy their craving.

'Another problem I envisage in your attempt to go into farming while you are away is derived from the mind-set of our people.

'As an employer, I pay my workers their due wages, expecting them to provide their labour in turn. That in my opinion should be the case whether I am present or away.

'Well, my impression is that many an employee does not see matters that way. They seem only to consider the benefit the employee gets from them. They seem to think they are sort of doing me a favour, helping to increase my wealth by virtue of their labour.

'So long as I am around they have no choice but to work the hours they are paid for. The moment I am not around, however, they adopt a lacklustre attitude.

'That is the reason why I spend as much of my time as possible on the farm when I am in the country. On not a few occasions, I have returned from a business trip to find the business in a mess.'

'That is a very peculiar attitude. How do we overcome it?'

'Well, your guess is as good as mine.'

I was enjoying every minute of the company of this extraordinary personality for whom I had the greatest respect.

I decided to raise the issue of lynching. It was a practice that was unimaginable in the Ghana I left behind thirteen years earlier. Yet it seemed to have become rampant. I had read about it on the Internet prior to our arrival. A few days after our arrival, the newsreader on one of the TV stations reported a total of four incidents nationwide.

'What has led to this change in the attitude of a tiny minority of a population generally credited with hospitality and detestation of any form of bloodshed?' I asked.

'Ghana, in the recent past, became a haven for people fleeing from several war-torn West African countries—Liberia, Sierra Leone, the Ivory Coast. While not putting the blame entirely on the doorsteps of the immigrants, a considerable increase in armed robbery and other violent crimes could be traced back to the arrival of that group of people.

'The population looked to the police for protection. Unfortunately, the impression the general population has in regard to the law enforcing officers is that of inability to protect them in the face of threat to life and property.

'The populace see the culprits they handed over to the police the day before for committing a crime the following day committing the same if not even more horrible ones. The perception that the police and to some extent the justice system are not doing enough to protect citizens has led some to take the law into their own hands to carry out these distasteful acts of self-justice.'

He paused for a while to respond to the ringing of his mobile phone. From what I gathered from the conversation, it appeared he had had to cancel an important meeting to play host to us!

'On the whole, however,' I remarked after he had ended the call, 'I think Ghana has made significant strides over the years.'

'Still," he nodded, "the cost of living is high compared to the earnings of the ordinary citizen. Everyone is trying in his or her own way to make ends meet.

'Many of those living in the countryside think a move to Accra will lead to a betterment of their situation. At the same time, those in Accra are looking beyond Ghana for an improvement in their situation.'

Just as he spoke his eyes caught sight of a group of his workers walking about fifty metres from where we were, on their way home after work.

'Do you see that young man in the middle, wearing the light blue shirt?' he began.

'Yes, I do,' I replied.

'Several months ago he approached me and said, "Well boss, I am afraid I will no longer be working for you as from next week."

'"What is the matter?" I inquired, very surprised.

'"I am travelling out of the country."

'"Where are you heading for?"

'"Europe."

'"You must be joking!"

'"No, I am not, boss."

'"What are you going to do there?"

'"I am in search of greener pastures!"

'"So you are not satisfied with the pay you get here?"

'"Well boss, one has to aim higher and higher in life!"

'"Tell me how you are going to get there!"

'"We are travelling by road through the Sahara Desert to Morocco. From there we shall continue by boat!"

'"So you are not alone?"

'"No, we are travelling in a group."

'"You must be aware of the risks involved. Have you thought them over carefully?"

'"Yes indeed; still, I have decided to go for it."

'Realising his mind was already made up, I could only wish him well for the future.

'Several weeks after that meeting I was in the office when someone knocked at the door. I opened it and to my surprise found him standing there in front of the door.

'"Am I seeing a ghost or a human being?" I remarked, completely taken aback.

'"A human being, boss!"

'"But I thought you were already in Europe?"

'"We attempted the journey, boss, but our vehicle crashed on account of the high sands of the Sahara!"

'He then told me of his horrifying experience.

'"We travelled first through Northern Ghana, crossed Burkina Faso and headed north," he went on. "Eventually we had to cross the Sahara. In the event we missed our way deep inside the vast, godforsaken wasteland. With no food and water around, we eventually resorted to drinking our own urine! Several in the group perished in the heat. It was distressing watching them perish.

"'Just as those of us still alive were bracing ourselves for a slow but certain death, we were discovered by some local herdsmen. They took us to their village, gave us something to eat and drink and also somewhere to lay our heads. As we soon realised, however, their help was not for nothing. Instead, they made us work for them over a considerable period of time in return for their assistance and hospitality. In the end they allowed us to go, giving us directions as to how to find our way back.

"'So I am back, boss. Like the biblical prodigal son, I have come to beg you to reinstate me.'

'Well, as you have noticed, I was merciful on him!'

At that juncture, I told him about the young man at Mim who was on his way to Singapore. 'You have to allow all who are willing to go to make their own mistakes. If you tell them the harsh realities of life in "Aburokyire", hardly any one of them will believe it. So let them go and leave us, the ageing ones, to stay behind!'

Just then Jonathan asked: 'I want to have a look at the animals.'

'Okay boy, come along, I will show them to you.'

Soon all of us were on our feet, heading for the wooden structure I referred to earlier on.

The rodents were kept in huge, rectangular wood-huts. Each occupied a compartment.

Feed in the form of grass was abundantly supplied.

During our schooldays we had hunted these rodents. Occasionally we came home with one or even a handful of them after we had inspected the traps we had set for the creatures. This, however, was the first time in my life that I saw them being kept domestically.

'How did you come by the idea to rear them?' I inquired from the man whose ingenuity seemed to have no bounds.

'While working on our farm, we managed to catch a few of them alive. The idea came to me not to kill them but rather to rear them. As you can now see for yourself, the stock has increased considerably, despite the fact that we feed on them regularly. Indeed they could easily be produced in large quantities to supplement the meat supply of the country.'

'Yet the price of food seems to be high in relation to the earnings of ordinary citizens.'

'What else do you expect, my friend, when the majority of the able-bodied youth have deserted the farmlands in the countryside in search of non-existent jobs in Accra and other towns and cities?'

From there we inspected the poultry. The stock numbered about two dozen. Finally we came to the goats! Jonathan's eyes brightened on seeing them. He was particularly fascinated by a large bearded billy-goat. All of a sudden he turned to our host.

'May I go inside and play with the goats?' he asked.

'Boy, they are not toys to be played with!' I replied.

'Please, please! Just for a few minutes,' he pleaded, looking at our host.

'Okay boy, you may do so if you wish.' With that our host opened the gate. No sooner had Jonathan stepped inside the yard than he began chasing the four-legged beasts around. As might be expected, they were not amused at the behaviour of the intruder and took to their heels. After pursuing the frightened creatures for about five minutes, we decided to bring their ordeal to an end.

'That is enough for today, boy!' our host cried out.

'You want me to come out?' the youngest member of the group, still busily pursuing the poor goats, inquired, the sweat pouring from his face.

'Yes, we need to go and inspect the pineapples!'

'Okay, okay!'

Moments later he joined the company of the rest of the group. Still panting for breath, he turned once again to our host.

'Where are the pineapples?' he asked.

'The main plantation is a few kilometres from here. I will take you there in my car.'

Soon all six of us were on board his pick-up, Jonathan and myself beside him, Rita, David and Karen at the back.

We returned to the main road and followed it in the direction that led away from Accra. After a distance of about half a kilometre we turned left to follow a bush path. Just as we were leaving the main road, Eddie turned to me and said, 'It may interest you to know that Michael Essien, the star of FC Chelsea Football Club and national hero hails from this area. If we had continued on the main road we would have driven past the village where he grew up; it is the first on the main road from here!'

On hearing the words Essien and Chelsea, Jonathan's eyes lit up. 'What did he say?' he asked me.

'I thought you heard him well.'

'Oh *you*! Please tell me!'

'Michael Essien was born in a village not far from here.'

'Really?'

'Yes indeed; do you enjoy watching him play?'

'Yes indeed he does,' I laughed. 'FC Chelsea is his team!'

'No, Manchester United!' he protested.

'That's typical, Jonathan. Sometimes he supports both teams: at other times he is for either the one or the other.'

'That's not true!' Jonathan protested.

'Which of the two do you support then?'

'Manchester United!'

'Your final word?'

'Yes indeed!'

'I hope that matter is settled for ever!'

'Yes it is.'

After driving about ten minutes along the path, we put the thick tropical vegetation behind us. Soon rows of pineapples came into view.

'Now you are seeing what you were yearning for.'

'But where are the *pineapples*?'

'You mean the fruits?'

'Yes.'

'What you see are the young plants. They are yet to bear fruit. I will take you to an area where you will see those already with fruit.'

On and on we drove, through the huge plantation. Ahead of us, on each side of the road along which we drove, lines of pineapples stretched as far as the eye could see. As we drove on we spotted a well-built man aged about thirty strolling along the space between two rows of the crop. On seeing us he waved.

'He is one of those who keep watch here, to guard against thieves and other intruders,' our host remarked.

After we had driven for a while, Eddie finally brought the vehicle to a halt. He turned to Jonathan and said, 'Get down boy! Now at last you will see what you've been longing for.'

After following him a distance of about one hundred metres, rows of the crop bearing large fruits, some of which had already turned yellow, came into view. They stretched several hundred metres ahead of us.

'Children, now just enjoy the scenery.'

It came to our notice that each fruits bore a small yellow plastic tag.

'What are they for?' Karen wanted to know.

'That is an indication that they are ready to be harvested this week. Several days prior to that some of the workers come round to make a mark on them and make an estimate of the weight of the harvest for that particular week. The figures are then transmitted to our customers well ahead of time.'

'Are the plants able to bear more fruit once a ripe fruit has been harvested?'

Karen wanted to know.

'No, each plant is harvested only once. Thereafter they are allowed to grow for a while. In due time a new shoot, suitable for replanting, springs up in the vicinity where the fruit was harvested. These are removed and preserved. The land is then cleared of the parent plants and prepared for re-cultivation with the shoots so won.'

'To be able to grow them on a commercial scale, I suppose one requires a large piece of land?' Rita queried.

'Yes, indeed. Not only that, one has to keep abreast with the times, in line with the changing demands of the market.'

'What do you mean by that?'

'Well, when I went into this business, our customers in Europe were happy with a type of pineapple prevalent here. In the course of time, the demand for that sort fell drastically in favour of a particular variety grown predominantly in South America!'

'Was it a way of squeezing the African farmer out of the market?'

'Your guess is as good as mine, friend! All of a sudden we were faced with the choice of either adapting to the dictates of the market or going out of business. Adapting involved money though, huge sums of money. That was required to import the seedlings from South America. Fortunately, I was able to raise the amount needed. That was not the case with the great majority of my colleagues; they had to call it quits. Today only a handful of us have managed to remain in business.'

Having satisfied the wish of the children we drove back to the main premises— not before we had taken several pictures of ourselves almost lost in a sea of countless plants of pineapple.

As we drove home that night, my prayer was that Heaven will send Ghana and, for that matter Africa, several men and women of Eddy's calibre—individuals bold enough to follow their convictions and ready to sail unchartered waters in their desire to realise their dreams, undeterred by what the world around may think of them; men and women who, having attained their goal after perseverance, hard-work and dedication, will continue to be rooted on the firm ground of modesty, not allowing pride and the feeling of having 'made it' in life carry them away.

CHAPTER 36
Scientific Multiplication

A few days prior to our departure for the UK we accompanied Nana on a visit to Dr Kwabena. Nana was keen on establishing the contact between his friend and I. As I learnt from him, Dr Kwabena returned to Ghana from the USA several years ago after becoming a specialist in the areas of Gynaecology and Obstetrics. He had in the meantime gained popularity in Ghana and beyond in the field of IVF treatment.

After some initial difficulty locating his street, we finally made it to his residence in the Airport Residential Area. Even before the transformation going on in Accra, that area of the city was known for its posh executive mansions. He lived on a large estate surrounded by thick concrete walls. The estate, like many others of a similar profile in the city, has a security post at the gate manned around the clock.

Nana introduced himself to the security.

'Boss is still at work.'

'I know that. I spoke to him earlier. He asked me to come about this time; he was hoping to be home by then.'

'It is possible he is stuck in traffic.'

'We would like to wait for him.'

On hearing that, he opened the gate and led us into a large living room on the ground floor of the three-storey building.

'You may wait for him here; I am sure it won't be long before he arrives.'

A young lady who introduced herself as Rita entered the room a few minutes later to serve us some soft drinks.

Not long after our arrival, Amma, his wife who assists her husband in the running of the clinic, arrived.

'Sorry, Nana, for keeping you waiting,' she said. 'You know how unpredictable this job is. Just as we were about to leave the clinic, he had to attend to a patient.'

Finally, about half an hour after our arrival, Dr Kwabena arrived. After excusing himself for keeping the traditional leader of his area waiting on him, he took his seat not far from where I was. After going through the formal tradition of *Amanebo, which* I referred to earlier on, the conversation became less formal.

'I did my basic medical training in the country,' he said after turning to me. 'I worked in various hospitals in the country after obtaining my qualification. In the process I met Amma, my wife. Later I moved on to the US to do a specialisation in Gynaecology and Obstetrics. After practising for a while thereafter, we decided to return home.

'At that time it was not an easy decision to take. Looking back, I do not regret we did. Over here one is among one's own people. Not only that—I am accorded a great deal of respect not only from my patients but by society in general.'

'I can imagine you have loads of work to do each day.'

'Indeed, particularly since I decided to go into the area of IVF treatment. Yes indeed, we operate a well-equipped fertility centre. You are free to visit us to find out things for yourself. You can also find more about us on the Internet. I will give you our web address later.' Just then his mobile phone rang.

'Excuse me a second,' he said and, stepping closer to the wall, he answered the phone. 'Oh, that is very unfortunate; very unfortunate,' he began, remaining silent as he listened. 'My goodness! My thoughts are with you. Do not give up hope!' (Silence.) 'Sometimes success comes only after several attempts.' (Silence.)

'I am confident success will crown our efforts. Please call the clinic tomorrow to book an appointment; we need to meet as soon as possible to consider our next move.'

'How is the demand for IVF treatment in the country?' I inquired after he had ended the call.

'Substantial, quite substantial. The number of the middle and upper class of our society is increasing. They are able and ready to pay for such treatment. Apart from Ghanaians, we receive a fairly large number of patients from other countries in the West African sub-region—Burkina Faso, Ivory Coast, Togo etc. As the saying goes, word spreads. Lady A, who has benefited from our treatment, tells Lady B about her experience who in turn passes the message on to Lady C.'

A well-functioning IVF clinic in Ghana! And a correspondingly substantial demand for the services by the populace! The country seems indeed determined to keep abreast with all aspects of life in the global village. Much as I would have liked to visit Dr Kwabena's clinic to see things for myself, unfortunately our heavy schedule prevented me from honouring the invitation.

A few days after our visit we were watching the evening news on TV when Rita drew my attention to a lady in the outfit of a golf player being interviewed.

'That is Amma!'

'Who is Amma?'

'Have you forgotten her so soon? I mean the wife of Dr Kwabena!'

'Yes indeed, that is she!' I replied after taking a closer look. 'Why is she on the TV news?'

'I don't know! You pay attention and listen.'

The reason soon became clear. She was being interviewed for having won an important Golf tournament organised during the weekend following our visit. Just then we recalled she had talked about an impending tournament during our visit. She was planning to inspect the course a few days prior to the event. Her effort at familiarising herself had clearly paid off, I said to myself.

CHAPTER 37
The Young Man who Lost His Way in the Courtyard of the Prominent

🙣

A few days prior to our departure I attended a meeting of MOBA 76, which is short for Mfantsipim Old Boys Association of the year 1976. After graduating from Oda Secondary School where I did my GCE Ordinary Level in 1976, I moved on to Mfantsipim School in Cape Coast to do a two-year GCE Advanced Level course. I graduated from there in June 1978.

Apart from the joy of meeting some of my mates, I wanted to ask KB, the current president of the association, to help establish contact between myself and the current Director General of the Ghana Education Service. I was desirous of bringing my two books *THE CALL THAT CHANGED MY LIFE* and *A LETTER TO MY DYING MOTHER: Survival in the West* to his attention. My aim was to talk to the key figure in the matters of formal education in Ghana about the possibility of adopting either both or one of them for use at the secondary school level in the country.

As I had earlier learnt from KB, the current Director General happened to be an Old Boy of our Alma Mater. He who has lived in Ghana for a while may probably be aware of the bond of solidarity that usually exists between individuals who attend or have attended a particular second level school. Although such solidarity is not restricted to the male sex, the term *old boy* rather than *old girl* is in common usage. Such bonds are usually so strong they overcome other social barriers such as that of ethnicity, religion, political conviction, etc. It is usually said that if an employer has to make a choice between two equally qualified applicants competing for a single vacancy, one an old boy/girl and the other not, the decision will likely fall in favour of the old boy or girl as the case may be.

The president directed me on the phone to the place where the fortnightly meeting was held. It was in the premises of the Retired Commissioned Officers Association, popularly known as the Veterans' Club. It boasted a large compound. He told me the meeting usually got underway around 19:00 hrs, but warned me not to expect everyone to be punctual since most will come directly from work. Lateness could be expected due to members having to work overtime or as a result of traffic congestion.

I was punctual. The Veterans' Club boasts two main buildings surrounded by a large fenced compound. The first of the two is located about fifty metres to the right of the entrance; the second is about a further-fifty metres to the left of the first.

At several locations on the large compound, long wooden tables surrounded by several wooden chairs had been placed where visitors could relax and also enjoy some drinks sold at a small kiosk at one corner of the compound.

After parking the bus on a parking lot within the gates of the building, I began to look out for the group. There was a handicap—I had not seen any of them since we parted from our boarding school almost twenty-nine years before. The problem was compounded by the fact that it had already turned dark. Instinctively, I headed for the building further away from the gate. Not only was it well lit, a handful of individuals had already gathered in a hall on the ground floor. It could be the group, I thought.

Just as I was about halfway towards it, an elegantly dressed elderly man caught up with me out of the blue and began to address me.

'Young man,' he said, 'you have definitely missed your way.' What did he mean by *young man*, I wondered? Admittedly, I am short in stature, reaching not much over 167cm above the earth's surface. I have also gone to some lengths to keep my weight just above what the scientists consider appropriate for my height. Still, I was not amused by the description 'young man'! Had he in the dark failed to notice the grey hair that was quite prominent on my head? Or perhaps he took me for one of the exceptional cases where grey hairs develop on the heads of some who have barely attained thirty years? I stared at him, not knowing how to respond.

'Indeed, you seem to be lost, young man,' he persisted. 'In any case, allow me to introduce myself. I am retired Army Officer Colonel Gbedemah.' (Did he mention a higher rank? I cannot recall precisely and apologise if I have inadvertently demoted him!) 'I joined the army when I was barely 18 years of age. I rose through the ranks to become a commissioned officer. Now I am enjoying my retirement.

'By the way, where you are heading for is strictly reserved for the prominent of our society. For example, that is where some candidates of the ruling NPP (New Patriotic Party) who are aspiring to win their Party's nomination to stand in next year's Presidential election met recently. They are individuals who are capable and also willing to pay a non-refundable fee of no less than 250 Million cedis or approximately 25000 US dollars to become eligible for the contest. I just mention this to illustrate that it is not a meeting place for the ordinary members of society! So I surmise that you are unquestionably lost.'

'Well,' I replied calmly, 'I am Dr Peprah-Gyamfi, a medical officer. I am here to attend a meeting of some old boys of Mfantispim School.'

On hearing my credentials, I noticed a significant change of attitude.

'Well, I do not know where they usually meet. You may ask one of the workers here. It is not in the direction you are heading for, however.'

As I turned to go, I reflected for a while on this unusual encounter. The elderly citizen seemed to be sunning in past glory, I thought to myself. Indeed, as a result of the rampant forceful take-over of the reins of government by the military, they used to wield power and influence in society, particularly during those times when they were in power. Ghana is now a stable and functioning democracy.

The military has a role to play as dictated by the democratic constitution, of course, but no more and no less. I will accord him respect by virtue of his age, as our society expects one to do to senior citizens of the community, but not on the grounds of the rank he attained whilst in the military.

Soon, someone who happened to be aware of the once fortnightly meeting directed me to an area where, according to him, the meetings were held. After waiting there about fifteen minutes, my mobile phone began to ring. It was KB on the line. He had just parked his car on the property and wanted to find out where I was.

Soon we were embracing each other. It was a pleasant meeting. At long last, I was meeting a group of people who would not demand anything form me, who would not require me to help solve any financial problems, who would not force me to think about any social plan of action.

The name *Mfantsipim* is and has always been a class of its own— even before the economic transformation that took place in the country. Only a few other schools in the country can boast a similar standing. To put it in perspective, it is like attending Eton or Harrow in England, or Gordonstoun School in Scotland, or the Boston Latin School in America. Needless to say, it has always been associated with the powerful of society.

The school, for example, prides itself of having produced ex-UN Secretary General Kofi Annan.

The gathering was informal and meant to maintain regular contacts between old boys of the class of 1976. As expected I was curious to know what the other old boys attending were doing for a living.

KB was doing very well, occupying a top position in an IT firm dealing in accountancy software. During the meeting he spoke about sending one of his children to study at a University in the United States. Preparations were almost complete, having met all the financial criteria demanded by the admitting University. Also present was the prefect of the famous school for the 1977/1978 academic year, popularly known by his alias Awo. He was still his noble self. To my question as to what he was doing for a living, he answered simply that he was shuttling between the US and Ghana on a regular basis, following the dictates of his business. He was visibly surprised to learn that I had not been to Ghana for almost thirteen years.

'Why so long, friend?'

'It was not intentional,' I replied. 'Circumstances beyond my control prevented me.'

I did not want to reveal to him that the main reason was financial. I wanted to save myself from embarrassment! He probably would have replied: 'Why continue living in cold and icy Europe when you can leave to settle in the African sun, especially if earning a living there is not that easy? After all, I, who live for the most part here, am able to fly at will to the US!'

There was also Okyne. He was the only person among the seven present whom I probably would have recognised on the street. He occupied a leading position at the Electricity Corporation in Ghana. He was a busy person, and no wonder, in view of the energy crisis. He had to stretch himself to be able to leave work early to attend the meeting.

After recounting several pleasant memories of our time at Kwabotwe, as the school is fondly referred to by its students, I begged permission to leave shortly before 22:00 hrs. The rest wanted to stay on for a while.

CHAPTER 38
Mechanical Failure on a Steep Decline

On Saturday 18th August I called my nephew, Taller, in the morning to find out how he and the other extended family members living in the crowded garage at Tema were faring. Taller is the eldest son of Edmund, my brother who is two years my senior. He had moved to Tema from Amantia a few years before to begin an apprenticeship in carpentry. He had in the meantime completed his training and was looking to me to help him establish a carpentry shop. He gained the alias Taller by virtue of his extraordinary height, rising to almost 195 centimetres. Since he was the most senior resident there, he had assumed the role of spokesperson of the community.

'I was about to call you, uncle,' he began on hearing my voice. 'I decided however to await the outcome of the X-ray examination before doing so.'

'What X-ray examination?' I inquired, taken aback.

'I mean the X-ray carried out on Shadrack.'

'On Shadrack? What is wrong with him?'

'He was involved in an accident late yesterday night.'

'In an accident!'

'Yes. He was involved in an accident when he was out driving a cab last night. He went to the A&E of Tema General Hospital for treatment. After examining him the doctors allowed him to go home. They instructed him to return today, should the chest pains he was complaining of worsen. On getting up this morning, he said the pain had intensified considerably so he decided to return to the hospital. I accompanied him.

The doctors have requested an X-ray. This has already been taken. We are presently awaiting the results.'

'How is his condition at the moment?'

'Well, not very bad, though he is still complaining of chest pains.'

'Any breathing problems?'

'I don't think so.'

'Extend my greetings to him and do not forget to call me as soon as you hear from the doctors.'

'Okay,doc!'

Shadrack injured driving a cab? During our visit to Tema the previous evening, I saw him busily engaged in polishing a saloon car which sported the typical colours of a Ghanaian taxi cab. We were in a hurry so I did not have the time to ask him about the vehicle. Apparently that was the vehicle he had been driving at the time of the accident.

I foresaw yet another financial burden coming my way, for as sure as the African sun would appear in the sky the next day, I was certain that my nephew Shadrack would not be in a position to meet the medical bill himself. The last child of my sister Donkor, who is two years my junior, he had recently been issued with a provisional licence. Instead of waiting a few more months for a proper licence before attempting to embark on commercial driving he had rushed into it with near catastrophic consequences.

Of course, his health was more important than financial considerations. In that respect I was thankful to God that, at least based on what I had heard from Taller, nothing life threatening had happened to him.

After waiting about two hours without hearing from him, I called Taller myself to find out the latest in regard to Shadrack.

'I was expecting your call,' he began

'But I thought you promised to call me as soon as the result of the X-ray was known.'

'I wanted to but unfortunately I did not have any credit.'

'Well, go ahead and tell me—what happened?'

'The doctor told him to go home because the X-ray was okay. He only gave him a prescription for some painkillers. We have in the meantime been to the chemist to buy them.'

'How much have you spent so far?'

'450000 cedis' (about 45 dollars). We used the money meant for food to settle it.'

'I will replace it when we meet tomorrow.'

Just as I was about to hang up Taller's voice reached me.

'That is not the end of the matter, uncle!'

'What do you mean by that?' I asked, exasperated.

'We need to tow the vehicle from the roadside. Otherwise he will be troubled by the police.'

'Have you spoken with the owner of the vehicle on that issue?'

'Yes. He says it is not his responsibility. He is even demanding that Shadrack pay for the cost of repairs.'

'On what basis did he give the vehicle out?'

'Usually a driver collects it fully tanked and returns it in that condition. Both agree on a daily amount that should be paid to the owner; the driver keeps whatever he earns above that amount.'

'We could use the bus to tow it.'

'Unfortunately that cannot be done, uncle.'

'Why not?'

'It is no longer legal to tow a broken-down vehicle in that manner. The law now requires one to engage the services of an officially registered towing service.'

'How much do you think would be required to do that?'

'Approximately 800000 cedis.' (Approximately 80 dollars.)

'Give me some time to think about all that.'

Yet another unexpected expenditure! There was no running away though—at least as far as the hospital and the towing bill were concerned. If I did not bear it, who else would?

Not so as far as the repair of the cab was concerned. I decided to leave him and the car owner to sort things out. The owner should normally have a comprehensive insurance to cover a vehicle he was using as a cab; he should blame himself if he didn't, I reasoned.

∗ ∗ ∗ ∗

There was one person I had not as yet met and who I needed to visit prior to our departure. Since the moment she got to know of our arrival in the country, Akua Dede, the eldest daughter of my sister Manu, had not ceased to flash my number. She was born just about the time I left Ghana in 1980 for Nigeria to embark on the adventure that finally saw me in medical school in Germany. Like many other people of her age, she had also moved to Accra to try her luck there.

She was in the meantime living with her husband and her little child in accommodation in the Darkoma district of the city. On Saturday 18th August, five days before our departure, we finally got the opportunity to visit her. Accra has a handicap that needs rectifying. Most of the streets in the city are unnamed, making it difficult not only to direct someone to a place but also for the person seeking a particular address to locate it. Anyone directing a person to a place has to be graphic—'Follow the Spintex Road from Tetteh Quarshie Roundabout. Drive straight for about eight kilometres until you see a newly constructed mainly glass building of the Standard Chartered Bank to the left. Continue on for about two more kilometres until you find a newly constructed Total Filling Station to the right. At that point, turn left unto the branch road directly opposite the filling station. Follow that road for about half a kilometre until the road comes to an end. From there turn left and follow the Muddy Road for about three hundred metres until you come to the Lena's Inn on the left.'

Whoa! Wouldn't it have been easier with something like Muddy Road 22, 1000 Accra 45? That definitely will be the challenge for the future. One way out of the situation is this: the government should consider allowing those who are financially in the position to do so to adopt the streets! They will make sure they are tarred and adequately lit. As compensation, the streets could be named after them. Until that time comes, however, my team and I had to find a way of getting to Akua Dede at Darkoma.

If it is not easy for one to find an address in a residential area such as Batsoona where the area is well planned with well-lain streets running between the buildings, one may well imagine how difficult it is for one to locate someone in a sprawling settlement in a place like Darkoma.

Fortunately, two residents of the garage at Tema knew the way— Shadrack as well as Adwoa, Akua's younger sister. I called Taller and instructed him to tell them to get ready. I would pick them up in the course of the afternoon and drive with them to Darkoma.

It was about 17:00 hrs when we set out from Tema. It took us almost two hours to complete a journey that in former times required less than half the time. The reason as usual was congestion, congestion, congestion! Even though the route did not pass through the central area of the city but through an area which in former times was sparsely populated, the streets even at this time of the day on a Saturday were choked with traffic and street vendors that severely hampered our progress. With some difficulty we were finally able to locate her accommodation.

Darkoma is a sprawling suburb to the south-west of the city. Akua rented a room in a small low-rise building which was typical of most of the buildings in the area. Residents have to cook their meals in the open space in front of the building and share the common toilet facility in a small building at one corner of the building.

Just as in the case of Joyce, I would have hardly recognised her on the street. She had developed into an attractive young woman bubbling with a lot of self-confidence. Unlike Joyce, she had not climbed the academic ladder, having left her schooling at the Junior Secondary School level. Even before my arrival in the country, news had reached me that she was engaged in street hawking. In her case, she was dealing in imported second-hand clothes, known locally as *Buroniwaawu*. I wanted to find out more about her trade.

'It is a hard life, uncle. I buy my clothes from dealers who buy in bulk and resell to petty traders like myself. I then carry them on my head and shoulders on the street. I am not aware of how many kilometres I cover each day; it is substantial, though.'

'Does the walking pay?'

'Well, it enables me to obtain my daily bread. My husband works as a fitter at a makeshift workshop. The resources we pull together just enable us to stay above water. If I could get sufficient capital to purchase the wares in bulk and distribute them to petty traders it would bring about a significant improvement in the business. It would also save me from walking kilometres every day in the scorching African sun looking for buyers.'

Yet another appeal for help, I said to myself.

'How much are you looking for?' I inquired after a while.

'Well, the clothes are imported in large bundles, each of which usually contains one particular piece of item. A bale may for example contain handbags for ladies, shoes for children, pairs of men's trousers, etc. Each bale costs at the moment three million cedis (approximately three hundred dollars). If you could help me with ten bales to start with, I would be very happy.'

'Thirty million cedis (three thousand dollars)!' I exclaimed. 'You are asking too much! You must be aware that you are not the only relative in need of help.'

'Well, the ball is in your court, uncle! You do what you can.'

'You will get three bales to start with; with some good management it could expand,' I promised her after careful consideration.

'Thank you very much, uncle. There is still an issue to consider. I need to hire a stall at the central market area where the items will be on display.'

'How much will that cost?'

'It depends on the size. One can however obtain one for about 100000 cedis a month. The problem though is that the owners normally demand anything from 12 months advance payment.'

'That is incredible!'

'That is the situation prevailing in this country. Tenants are required to make several months' payment in advance for whatever they want to rent—be it a house, a flat or, as in this case, a stall. One has to reckon with a minimum of twelve months. In some cases, property owners demand as much as three years advance payment.'

'But that is unacceptable! What is the government doing about it?'

'The government? Well, it is possible laws exist to protect the interests of the tenant. Who cares in a situation when demand exceeds supply?'

'Okay, you go around looking for one; I will help you with the initial money needed to rent it.'

Just as we were about to leave, electricity was restored to the area.

'Good!' Akua said. 'The light has been restored. I can now show you our room.'

I was lost for words when I stepped into the room. It was barely three metres wide and three metres long! A wooden bed at one corner had taken a considerable part of the space. Much of the rest was filled with their belongings. She shared it not only with her husband and their three-year-old child, but also with her teenage brother as well as the eight-year-old daughter of an extended family member she was caring for because her mother had fallen severely ill.

'How are you able to survive in this accommodation?' I inquired.

'We are managing, uncle,' she replied, a broad smile on her face.

We ended our visit after about half an hour and headed back to the hotel. Just as I was pondering over my visit and how best I could help Akua, Taller, who had taken his place on the passenger's seat beside me, turned to me and said, 'Uncle, I hope you have not forgotten the need to tow the vehicle. Shadrack is in danger of being called upon to pay a heavy fine should the police come across it.'

'How much did you say would be required?'

'A minimum of 800,000 cedis (about 80 dollars), uncle. Even then we would have to do some hard bargaining.'

'Okay, you can arrange to have it towed. I will give you the amount involved as well as the hospital fee when I drop you.'

Just then it occurred to me that Taller had told me the previous day that according to Shadrack it was not his fault that the accident had occurred. Instead, he placed the blame on the other driver involved. That being the case, why were they not holding him to account? I decided to find out the truth from the horse's own mouth.

'Shadrack, now that you are recovering from the initial shock of the accident, could you let us know how it all happened?'

'Well, it was due to my brakes,' he began in his usual soft voice.

'What happened?'

'They failed me.'

'But you told Taller it was not your fault?'

'Well, now you know the truth. I was descending a slope. Suddenly the lights turned red. The large lorry in front of me stopped. I applied my brake. But it wouldn't work!'

'What about the handbrake?'

'It was not working and I was already aware of it. I saw death staring me in my face. Before me was the large truck; parked by the roadside in a no-parking area directly in front of the traffic light was a mini-bus. I saw two alternatives, either to drive straight and crash under the lorry, or swerve to the right and crash into the parked vehicle. The latter appeared to me to be the lesser of two evils so I crashed into it.'

'That was a near escape.'

'Yes indeed! I really saw death staring me in the face. Despite all the problems confronting me, I did not want to die young, so I did my best under the circumstances. Indeed if I had not avoided the truck, I would have driven straight under it, in which case you would now be thinking of how to dispose of my body rather than paying for my hospital bill.'

'So the accident was caused by you, not a third party as I was originally told?'

'That is the truth of the matter. Fortunately for me the driver of the mini-bus, fearing the police would question him for parking in a strictly forbidden area, drove away rather than confront me with the repair for the damage caused to his vehicle. Though not substantial, it will still cost him quite a good deal of money to put things right.'

'Were there any passengers in your cab?'

'Yes, a young couple I had picked up a few minutes before the accident. Fortunately they escaped unhurt.'

'Were you unaware of the problem with the brakes before you set out to work?'

'Well, the owner told me about it. He made it clear though that he did not have the money to put things right. The agreement was for me to use my own resources to put things in order. I would have deducted the amount involved from the earnings that were due to him. Since I did not have enough money, I only carried out a partial repair. I thought that would be enough for the night. I would have done the rest the next day. As it turned out, that was not enough.' I gave them the money they had requested to enable them to I tow the vehicle the next day.

They did not wait even for the next morning. As I learnt later, they called a towing firm immediately they got home. They carried out the transaction that very night. As far as the repair of the vehicle was concerned, the owner promised to do so. Shadrack would bear half the cost. This would be deducted from his future earnings.

CHAPTER 39
A Chinese Lady Feeling Good in Ghana

I t was now Sunday 19th August. We were left with four days before our return to the UK. There were still several relatives in the Accra-Tema area to see, not just for the sake of seeing, but as usual to listen to their problems and do what we could to help.

First we called on Rita's relations living at the Teshie-Nungua Estates in Accra, in the house where she used to live with her late uncle and his German wife. As I mentioned earlier on, the building is occupied by several members of her extended family who had moved to the national capital for various reasons.

Needless to say, we were heartily welcomed. They had invested their scarce resources to prepare a delicious meal. The story of Emma, Rita's cousin in particular, was pathetic. Despite experiencing chronic joint pains, she had to get up every day to walk long distances to try to sell her wares on the street.

'Still, we are surviving—by His grace!' she said, pointing to the Heavens.

The next day, Monday, 20th August,was the turn of Nana Kwame, the relative we had originally planned to pick up at Akim Oda. He rang the day after our return to the capital to find out about us and to remind us about our promise to him. In the end it was arranged that he should travel to Tema that Sunday to spend the night at the already crowded garage.

The next day, Monday, I would pick him up and travel with him to purchase the machine in question—a spraying machine used to spray various wood protection devices.

I picked him up early in the morning from Tema. I asked Taller, who knew in which part of Accra we could obtain the said machine, to accompany us.

We parked the bus a fair distance from the central area of the city to avoid congestion. We then followed Taller through the busy streets of the city. Finally, after about twenty minutes' walk, we came to an area where several shops dealing with small machines and electrical equipment were located.

After having failed to agree on the price in two shops, we entered a third one. I was positively surprised, for the price quoted by the sale assistant, 1.8 million cedis (approximately 180 dollars) was far below what the others had been demanding. Even then I decided to do some bargaining.

'I will buy it for 1.2 million cedis,' I told the assistant.

'No, Sir. Our last price is 1.6 million cedis,' he replied. Just before I could react to the offer, a door leading to a room at the back of the shop opened. Out stepped a woman aged about forty, whom I later learnt to be from China.

'How is the stand of things?' she inquired from the sale attendant.

'He has offered 1.2 million.'

'What are we demanding?'

'1.6 Million.'

She then turned to me. 'Okay, sir,' she began in accented English, 'you are our first customer for today so we want to make a special offer—1.4 million. That is our final offer.' I agreed to the offer. Just as I was handing the money to the sales attendant, I turned to her and asked, 'Ghana good?'

'Yes, yes, Ghana good!' she replied, a broad smile on her face. Just then my mobile phone rang—and just as I went for it, it went dead.

'Missed call' appeared on the small screen of the device. Soon I knew who had flashed me—it was Akua Dede. I knew it would be in connection with the *buroniwaawu* business so I called back without delay. Time was not on my side. I wanted to make as many people happy as I could prior to my departure.

'What is burning, Akua?' I inquired.

'I have found a stall being offered for rent. Could we please arrange to view it?'

'Where is it?'

'At Kantamanto market. Indeed, I am at the stall right now trying to agree on a price with the owner.'

I knew Kantamanto market was in the central area of Accra. It could not be far from where we were. Yet I wanted to get a confirmation from Taller.

'Yes indeed,' he replied, 'it is barely one kilometre from where we are.' On hearing that I instructed her to wait for us. We would call back as soon as we were finished with Nana Kwame.

Next, we bought several accessories that he would need for the machine. Finally, we put him on a taxi and asked the driver to take him to the central lorry station about three kilometres away. There he would find a bus that would take him back to Akim Oda.

'All the best, friend! That concludes what I can do for you. Your assignment is to help your mother support your other nine siblings!'

I began to laugh in my head. How could I expect that young man to fulfil his obligations by virtue of a single wood-spraying machine! For the moment, at least, I congratulated myself for having fulfilled my social obligation towards him. That turned out to be premature though, for my nephew turned to me and said, 'That is not all, uncle. You know I learnt the trade from someone else. Tradition requires that at the end of it all, I pay him some money and also offer him some drinks. In his case he is demanding two million cedis as well as a large billy-goat and a crate of minerals!'

Indeed, I recalled that his mother had mentioned something about this on a previous occasion.

'Okay friend,' I replied, 'you just accept what you have got today. Give me approximately four weeks. I will send you enough money to enable you to fulfil that obligation. Give me a call to remind me should you fail to hear from me after the expiry of that period.'

He did not forget one detail of my promise! Exactly four weeks after our return, our phone rang one evening. When I picked it up I recognised his voice.

'Sorry for bothering you, uncle, but you asked me to call you to remind you about your promise!'

There was no running away! Two days later I sent him the money in question. While still in Ghana I did wonder how that young man would be able to face the challenges of his business by virtue of only a small wood-spraying machine. At the time, though, I was congratulating myself for the good work done. Afterwards a cab took Taller and me to the Kantamanto market. After some initial difficulties, we located Akua at a place we had agreed upon. She led us through narrow alleys and passageways. On each side of the narrow way, hawkers offering all sorts of items—pairs of trousers of all makes and sizes, T-shirts, shirts, shoes, belts, necklaces, chains—were lined up. She led us to an area lined with wooden stalls of various sizes in each of which was a trader selling *buroniwaawu*. Finally she stopped at one of them.

'I have brought my uncle,' she told the occupant, a woman whose age I put at around thirty.

'Tell your uncle what we have agreed on. I do not want to repeat what I have already told you.'

'Well, she is demanding a rent of 100000 cedis per month. I am required to pay twenty-four months rent in advance.'

'Young woman, in my opinion twenty-four months advance is too much to demand. I can offer 18 months—1.8 million ready cash.' I pointed to the bag I was keeping a firm hold on.

'Well,' the woman relented, 'for the sake of Akua who I regard as my sister, I will agree to the offer.'

Soon I was counting the money I had withdrawn from a cash machine earlier on.

'Akua, you must be proud of your uncle,' the young woman remarked as I handed her the money. 'Now it is yours for the next eighteen months. I will pack my items by the end of the weekend.'

Being curious by nature, I wanted to find out why the woman had decided to give up her stand.

'I want to join my husband in Italy,' she replied. 'He has been gone a few years now. It is about time I joined him.'

I could read the joy in her eyes as she said that.

'What is he doing there?'

'He is employed as a factory hand,' she said. 'Akua tells me you are also in Aburokyire.'

'That is correct.'

'Where?'

'In the UK.'

'How is life in Aburokyire?'

'What has your husband told you?'

'He says he is okay.'

'What then do you expect from me? Every country in Aburokyire is different, so even if I tell you what life is like in the UK, it won't be useful to you since you are heading for Italy. In any case I wish you all the best for the future.'

Kwadwo, the good friend I got to know during my days at Oda Secondary School, had spent several years living in Italy. He had on several occasions reported back about the difficult conditions under which Ghanaians and other migrants from other parts of the developing world living there were exposed to. It was not my duty to poison the expectations of someone burning to be united with her husband by revealing that to her. After all, he could be part of the fraction that makes up the exception to the rule.

Having spared Akua the problem of paying rent for the next eighteen months, the next thing left was the 9 million cedis (approxiamtely 920 dollars) needed for the three bales. I promised to hand this sum to her at the airport on Thursday, just before our departure.

Several years before, I had given her mother substantial capital to begin a trade. Things went very well at the beginning, but just as her business began to flourish the unexpected happened—her husband fell seriously ill. In the end his problem was a double blow to her; not only did the sickness eat deeply into her capital, but her efforts could not prevent his death. In the end she was left alone to cater for their four children with a completely depleted capital. It was my prayer that she would be spared the misfortune.

There was the last beneficiary to consider regarding the 'social packet' in my pocket. Donkor, the sister who follows me directly on the family tree, has four children—Elijah, Deborah, Rachael and Shadrack. Those familiar with the Holy Bible will know that the four names are those of four prominent figures in the Old Testament. Indeed, she used to be married to a pastor of a church at Amantia. A curious thing about the church was that the members left the rest of the villagers behind and went to settle at the outskirts of the village, about half a kilometre away from the rest of the villagers—for they did not want to become contaminated by the sins of the rest of the village, or so they reasoned.

Somewhere along the line, my brother-in-law nevertheless fell victim to the lusts of the flesh they thought they could overcome by leaving the rest of the village behind, by having an affair with one of the women of the congregation. Eventually he was suspended from the congregation. Later he completely turned his back on the church, got divorced from Donkor and married his new lover.

Deborah, Donkor's daughter, was the intended beneficiary of my last 'social packet.' When I last visited Ghana she was barely ten years old. In the meantime she had grown up into a captivating young woman. About three years before our visit, her father was approached by a wealthy lady from Muronaamu, Amantia' s immediate neighboour to the north, about five kilometres away, to ask for the hand of Deborah in marriage to her brother. She was on a visit from Germany where she was resident and was concerned that her brother who had come of age was not finding a suitable woman to marry. It was a very unusual happening since arranged marriages within the Akans group, to which we belong, has become very rare.

Was it because the whole matter was initiated by the prominent visitor from Aburokyire?

In any case, my brother-in-law agreed to the proposition against the expressed will of his daughter. Nevertheless Deborah reluctantly left Amantia to be with his husband at Muronaamu.

Her sister-in-law kept her promise and acted as the main source of financial support for the married couple. Unfortunately, shortly before our arrival, she died suddenly in Germany.

During our first visit to Mpintimpi, Donkor told me one of her children had absconded to Accra, leaving her two young children with her. Owing to the excitement surrounding our visit, I did not find the time to question her in detail about the matter at the time.

When I visited the 'garage community' on our return to Accra, she approached me.

'I am Deborah, one of the children of your sister Donkor,' she began.

'What are you doing here? Your mother told me you have left, leaving your children behind.'

'I did not sense any prospect of progress in the village so I decided to leave.'

'Who will take care of your children?'

'Mother, of course,' she smiled.

'But I understand you are married?'

'My father "sold" me into marriage: I cannot bear it any longer.'

'So what are your immediate plans?'

'I want to begin an apprenticeship in hairdressing.'

At this point I knew what was boiling in the pot. When it came to cashing in on her marriage, her father was quick to stretch out his hands. When it came to paying for her to learn a trade, the 'rich' uncle from Aburokyire was being consulted.

'Have you found someone who will take you on?'

'Yes, indeed. We have found a well-known hairdressing saloon in this area. The owner has agreed to take me on. I have to pay a one-off fee of three million cedis to be admitted.'

I decided to give her the chance to learn a trade that could lead to an improvement in her life.

Just the day prior to our departure, accompanied by Taller and herself, we called on the proprietress of the stylist shop.

She was not what I expected. She handed us a formal contract of engagement she insisted should not be signed that day. Instead she asked us to take it home and read it carefully and return it signed the following day only if we were in agreement with its contents. It was her stipulation that we looked over the contract at home first before returning it signed the next day. That was the first time I had heard someone in Ghana require an apprentice to formally sign a contract of engagement before beginning a period of training. Or had the rules changed in the meantime?

When she was told that I was leaving the country the next day she agreed to make an exception in our case. After signing as guardian, I handed her the 3 million cedis training fee.

Just as I was about to drive away, Deborah's brother Shadrack, who had just witnessed the signing ceremony and the subsequent payment, approached me.

'Uncle,' he said, 'what about the damaged taxi? How am I going to get it repaired?'

On hearing that I nearly exploded with fury!

'You people want to squeeze me to the point of personal bankruptcy!' I shouted in exasperation. 'I have paid for your hospital bill and the towing fee. You go and sort out the rest with the cab owner!'

CHAPTER 40
Damaged in Transit

S omeone has said that he who travels home to Ghana to visit relations
should take one important precaution, namely to travel with a return
instead of a one-way ticket.

The reasoning is that, no matter how much money one takes along
on such a visit and also no matter how careful one is in spending one's
money, unforeseeable events, problems, circumstances, etc., relating to
the extended family could lead one spending the very last penny on
such a trip. Without a return ticket, one might well end up stranded
indefinitely.

As we went about trying to solve one problem after the other, our one
consolation was that when push comes to shove we still had our return
tickets to fall back on to enable us to escape the battlefield for a period
to return to the UK to work in order to replenish our depleted savings.

The return flight was scheduled to take off 16:10 hrs local time.
Aware of the congestion on the Spintex Road, we left home well ahead
of time. It was just as well that we did, for we were stuck in the traffic
of the Spintex Road for almost an hour.

Several members of our various families including of course Akua
Dede to whom I had promised the capital for the *Buroniwaawu* business
gathered at the Airport to bid us goodbye. After calling her aside so as
not to attract the attention of the rest, I handed her 9 million cedis (900
dollars) which I had wrapped in a small polythene bag.

'That is what the Germans call *HILFE ZUM SELBSTHILFE* (aid
meant to assist you to help yourself). That is my lifelong help for

you. Keep it well and use the earnings to assist other members of the extended family.'

With tears of gratitude in her eyes, she concealed the bag in her handbag. Soon we joined the rest of the group.

What about the bus? One will surely want to know.

I placed it in the care of a trusted associate. Earlier on he had recommended a middle-aged man who, according to him, was a good driver and a man of integrity. Though the proceeds were meant for the upkeep of the extended family, I chose not to entrust it to any of them. Past experience of several of my Ghanaian patients in Düsseldorf led me to that step. Not only did the vehicles they had entrusted to their relations lead to intrigues, quarrels and what-have-you; in some instances the caretakers had acted according to the prevailing philosophy of our society that has it that 'what belongs to my brother/sister belongs to me'—and in the end they had squandered the earnings obtained from running the vehicle.

We finally bade goodbye to our relations and headed for the departure lounge. In former times, departure and arrival was by means of a single building. Now a newly constructed building complex just a few metres from the former served as the point of departure.

The short flight to Lagos was uneventful.

Our connecting flight to London was not due for about five hours. In due course I began to feel thirsty. After a short search I discovered a drinking fountain where several transit passengers had gathered. Just then it occurred to me that we had no Nairas—Nigeria's national currency—on us. I had a credit card but there happened to be no ATM machine in the area. What was to be done? I approached the sales assistants to find out whether I could use my credit card.

'Unfortunately not,' she replied. 'We do accept Euros, dollars and pounds, however.'

Poor me, I had exchanged all my pounds in Ghana!

As usual Rita had thought about the eventuality and had kept a twenty-pound note. Eventually we bought drinks that amounted to about five pounds. I handed the note to the sales assistant, thinking she would have no difficulty with the change. That was not to be the case. Instead she looked at me in surprise and asked, 'No five or ten pound note?'

'No, sorry.'

'Well, please take a seat as I look for change.'

She then went from table to table asking those gathered there for help. After a while she returned.

'Unfortunately I am not able to change your money.'

Just as I was about to return the drinks for my money, she asked unexpectedly,

'Sir, will you accept dollars as your change?'

'Brilliant!' I replied, happy about the prospects of being able to quench my thirst. 'How much will that come to?'

'Wait a moment as I calculate.' After a short while she turned to me.

'Twenty-seven dollars.'

Soon I was on my way back to the rest of the group with twenty-seven dollars and enough drinks to go round.

Contrary to our expectations, David was unusually calm as we waited for our flight. Finally, approximately an hour before the flight, we made our way to the departure gate.

On producing our boarding passes one of the officers looked at me.

'You are the passengers in transit from Accra, aren't you?'

'Yes indeed.'

'I have been waiting for you.'

'What is the matter?' I inquired in astonishment.

'Unfortunately there has been a problem with your luggage.'

'What problem?'

'Somehow the zip of one of the pieces of your luggage got damaged in transit!'

'How?'

'One of you should please follow me downstairs to ascertain whether something is missing before we put it on board,' he continued, ignoring my question. I asked the rest to wait while I accompanied the officer.

My thought on seeing the damage done was unequivocal—someone determined to access its contents had deliberately tampered with it. Because it had been padlocked, the culprit had obviously made use of a sharp instrument to cut it open a few centimetres along the entire course of the zip. I nervously inspected the contents. As I did so, I wished it was Rita, not myself who had to do so, for it was she who had done the parking. Still, as far as I could make out, nothing had gone missing.

The officer breathed a sigh of relief on hearing that. Next, he took a large plastic bag from a trailer. With the help of myself and another officer, we placed the damaged bag into it. He finally sealed it with sellotape. As I returned to the rest of the group, the conversation I had with Kwasi on arriving in Ghana echoed in my mind.

'When I got your e-mail to the effect that you were flying with Virgin Nigeria instead of Lufthansa, I began to pray to the Lord to help preserve your luggage.'

'Why?'

'Only recently one of my friends who flew with that airline lost part of his luggage on transit in Lagos. Though they boast good planes and a good service, they seem to have problems with the safety of their luggage, particularly in regard to the flight that goes through Lagos.'

The rest of the family were relieved on hearing that the contents were intact. We decided however to demand a replacement of the damaged suitcase on our arrival in London.

Finally, at about 2100 local time, the huge Boeing lifted up from Lagos International Airport.

We were informed just before departure that we would make an unscheduled stopover at Abuja, the administrative capital of the most populous nation on the African continent, to refuel, making me wonder whether the airport of the commercial capital had run out of fuel.

Not long after the flight, I fell into a deep sleep to be awakened only by the jerking and rumbling associated with the landing at Abuja.

After waiting about forty-five minutes we finally embarked on the final leg of the journey.

Jonathan who sat beside me was so exhausted he could hardly remain awake to enjoy the delicious meals served. Since we had hardly eaten anything since we had our breakfast at Lena's Inn, I took advantage of the little boy's exhaustion to fill my stomach to the very full!

After about five hours into the flight, the announcement from the cockpit filled the plane: 'Please fasten your seatbelt for a descent to London Gatwick. It is a wet and chilly morning in London, local temperatures around 10 degrees Celsius. Thank you for flying with us and we look forward to welcoming you on board in the future.'

On hearing this about the prevailing weather, I grew furious with myself and wished I had remained back in the African sun! I knew that was wishful thinking, though. For the next few years, at least, partly on account of the education of the children and partly because of the need to build up a substantial capital base that was needed not only for the survival of our nuclear family but also to meet some of the social responsibilities highlighted so far, I had no alternative but to come to terms with the inclement British weather.

The huge man-made bird was brought smoothly to earth by the able hands of the man on the helm of this technological wonder. After saying goodbye to the friendly crew we headed for the immigration and passport control.

The first thing I did after collecting our luggage was to head straight to a counter of the Airline to launch a complaint concerning the damaged suitcase. They were very forthcoming and promised to replace it in the near future. They kept their word and sent us a new suitcase which happened to surpass the old in looks and quality!

CHAPTER 41
Three Cheers for Ghana!!!

As we drove back to Loughborough, occasionally stuck in the busy morning rush-hour traffic, much of my thoughts were still on Ghana, hovering between Accra, Mpintimpi, Mim, Amantia and back to Accra.

I began to recount the experiences of the last five weeks. Ghana no doubt was undergoing a period of rapid transition. In such period of social and economic change there is bound to be winners as well as losers.

The saying that an individual viewing a bottle filled to the middle with water could describe it as either half-empty or half-full came to mind. How did I personally view the situation in Ghana, based on my five-week stay?

Should I give prominence to the enormous challenges still facing the country—unemployment, the high cost of living, poverty, disease, crime, etc., and consider the bottle Ghana as half-empty? Or should I take a more optimistic view and describe the bottle Ghana as half-full?

Well, I decided I have every reason to take the latter view! Indeed, despite the enormous challenges still facing the country, I could sense the breeze of hope and optimism blowing over the country, being part of the same winds of change that led black Africa to political independence.

Although I have been away from the country for a while, I lived the first twenty-five years of my life almost uninterruptedly in the country. It is based on my experience from those days that my present optimistic feeling that all is going to turn out well for the country is grounded.

231

Indeed, my own personal experience of living the first twenty-five years of my life in that country has led me to that conclusion. Apart from the pleasant memories of my early childhood days when we went to school to learn patriotism and returned home with smiling faces to show our parents the several new textbooks, new exercise books, plenty of chalk, a slate to write on, all provided free by the Nkrumah regime, I had few pleasant memories of the country to write about— until my recent visit. Whatever our learned historians might make of the first civilian administration under Dr Kwame Nkrumah, the coup that overthrew that regime in 1966 was unquestionably a harbinger of an unfortunate condition in the country's history—political instability.

The military, once they had tasted power, never seemed to be satisfied with its main role—that of defending the country against outside threat. Thus the military intervention or *coup d'etat* of 1966 ushered in a sad and vicious cycle followed by a handover to a civilian administration only to be followed by another military takeover.

Political instability led to economic downturn, since understandably hardly anyone was inclined to invest in a climate of uncertainty.

Towards the end of the 1970's, the economic situation in the country was so desperate that anyone who was capable of doing so found a way to escape the hardships. It was during those days that the term *OGYAKROM—the town on fire* was coined to describe the harsh economic reality prevailing in the country. For me personally, my active involvement in the suffering of the population came to an end when I left the country at the beginning of December 1980 for Nigeria. My fellow countrymen who stayed behind, and who experienced the traumatic events following the early years of the Rawlings regime, are in a better position to tell their own story.

It is in the light of the above that the reader might understand my tendency, perhaps, to have been carried away, delighted, by the impressive developments I observed, not only on the economic front but also in the area of personal liberty and freedom of speech.

Not only is the country now enjoying political stability, but there are mechanisms in place to prevent the abuse of individual rights, to check accountability and foster greater transparency in government, to prevent acts of bribery and corruption, embezzlement of public funds, etc., from going unchecked.

The Commission on Human Rights and Administrative Justice (CHRAJ) has been set up not only to promote and protect human rights, based on the guide- lines of the Paris Principles, but also to see to administrative justice and take over the function of Ombudsman. CHRAJ also has an anti-corruption mandate. The Public Accounts Committee (PAC for short), a parliamentary subcommittee, for example, has been set up to enforce accountability in the system, in particular in regard to officials in Ministries, Departments and agencies entrusted with the use and management of public funds and other resources. The Serious Fraud Office (SFO) was created by an Act of Parliament in 1993 to, among other things, investigate any suspected offence provided for by law, which appears to have reasonable grounds to involve serious financial or economic loss to the State or to any organisation or institution in which the State has financial interest. The three institutions are not only extant on paper but have been vigorous in their pursuit of their respective roles to the benefit of the country.

The press is also free to operate within the norms of a free and civilised society. Unlike previous times, holders of public office are constantly made aware of the fact that there is a 'Big Brother' watching over them.

While not passing judgement on the matter, the fact that the issue surrounding the so-called Hotel Kufuor came to the fore and was energetically pursued not only by the opposition and the press, but by the general public, shows how much freedom of expression is enjoyed in today's Ghana.

Admittedly, the cost of living is high compared to the earning of the average worker. Unfortunately the issue of disparity between average earnings and the cost of living is not new in Ghana. It is not without reason that many have in the past referred to the Ghanaian as a magician capable of surviving on a monthly earning which in some instances could be as little as about a fifth of his/her monthly expenditure. Is this perhaps one of the general characteristics of a developing world?

There is indeed the need to produce abundant and cheap food locally to feed the populace. There is a marked difference today from the situation that used to prevail in the country. During the difficult days of the late 1970's and, for that matter, much of the 1980's, even if one had the money, food could be difficult to come by. At the moment however food items abound though at quite high prices.

In my opinion it should not, at least in the long run, be acceptable that a piece of chicken should sell for about three times the minimum wage of the worker. Chicken should after all not be regarded as a luxury but a basic food item that should be affordable to the average worker.

Despite the challenges facing the country, Ghana, which led black Africa to political independence, is bravely marching forward with the front-runners for political freedom and economic development on the continent.

In a situation where the name 'Africa' is generally associated with everything that is bleak and negative, indeed, in the context of a continent generally linked with dictatorship, corruption in high and low places, hunger, disease, war, conflict and everything desolate and hopeless, any light in such a bleak environment needs to be kept glowing with fuels of encouragement rather than put down by words of disheartenment and dismay. It is in the light of this that I urge all men and women of goodwill towards Ghana in particular and Africa in general to join me in a resounding salute in recognition of the dramatic progress this country, this forerunner, this beacon of light, has made:

THREE CHEERS FOR GHANA!

www.ingramcontent.com/pod-product-compliance
Lightning Source LLC
Chambersburg PA
CBHW051818090426
42736CB00011B/1534